THE IMPLICATION OF HUMAN, INCORPOREAL EXISTENCE

By Julian Hamer

© All rights reserved. No part of this publication may be reproduced without the prior permission of the author.
First published, 2014 - Revised, 2020

Dedicated to my beautiful wife Ellen

Dedicated to my beautiful wife Clair

THE IMPLICATION OF HUMAN, INCORPOREAL EXISTENCE

The Overlooked Significance of the Intangible and Qualitative Dimension of Existence

By Julian Hamer

CONTENTS

    INTRODUCTION P1
1. THE HUMAN IPSEITY P7
2. STRAIGHTFORWARD COGNITION P13
3. INTRINSIC VALUE P21
4. INTRINSIC EXISTENCE P21
5. HUMAN INCORPOREAL EXISTENCE P41
6. SUBSTANTIVE SIGNIFICANCE P49
7. PREJUDICED CONVICTION P57
8. TRUE, FALSE – REAL, UNREAL
9. THE SIGNIFICANCE OF CONTENT P71
10. IMMEDIACY P79
11. THE QUALITATIVE DISTINCTION P89
12. IMMEDIATE ENGAGEMENT P99
13. EXPERIENTIAL ENCOUNTER P105
14. INTELLECTUAL MINIMIZATION P111
15. THE THIRD COGNITIVE APPROACH P117
16. THE AUTHENTIC HUMAN CONDITION P123
17. CONCLUSIVE KNOWLEDGE P129

Other books by the same author P137

x

INTRODUCTION

The difference between conventional cognitive practice and immediate engagement lies in the existential significance of our human uniqueness. Preoccupied with our thoughts and feelings, we overlook the relevance of our own unique existence. Consequently, we fail to recognize that within the condition of the singular nature of our identity, there essentially resides the capacity of immediate cognition.

Even if we only casually observe the functioning of the human intellect and of our feeling-sentience, we must recognize and conclude that they evaluate and assess information only indirectly and ambiguously. We find, consequently, that we may be readily convinced and subsequently take a position that is without merit, if the argument is sufficiently persuasive. That is to say, while the evidence may seem to be irrefutable, our conclusions will inevitably remain inconclusive and readily undermined upon contradiction.

Our intellectual, evaluative processes involve the logical rearrangement of information, founded upon accumulated and current justification. That is, we evaluate a situation abstractly and obliquely, before or after the cognitive event.

Human feeling-sentience is similarly inadequate in terms of cognition. Inevitably and necessarily, it is only a subjective faculty and it is unable to decisively offer definitive knowledge concerning the nature of the existence of phenomena.

While reason serves us well as an indirectly functioning, evaluative discipline and our corporeally dominated feelings allow us to appraise a situation and determine its personal value to us, neither of these cognitive practices offer conclusive knowledge. It is true that the intellect approaches decisiveness when it is occupied mathematically because it ideally calculates and enumerates. But, we must scrupulously reduce and quantify evidence in order that we may evaluate it more effectively by estimation and thereby approach a conclusive result.

Unfortunately, qualitative significances are irreducible and when we attempt quantification we inevitably lose the intrinsic value of the phenomenon, and subsequently, solely represent the tangible appearance. We imagine that we have thereby garnered the entirety, but, in reality, we merely distill blatant, peripheral and exclusively quantifiable material properties into convenient numerical terms.

This is a significant shortcoming of the human, cerebral faculty. In particular, it cannot conclusively reason and logically evaluate incorporeal values because it cannot justify intangible intelligence. In other words, rationale deals effectively with tangibly verifiable data, but it cannot manage elusive information whose existence can only be confirmed experientially. Needless to say, the intellect has to assume that intangible and physically unverifiable evidence is unjustifiable in a manner similar to fiction.

The point may be illustrated if we select the example of two tomatoes, the one cultivated artificially while the second is germinated in organic soul and the fruit, sun-ripened. Upon physical analysis, both vegetables are found to be identically composed and even genetically indistinguishable because it is their material properties alone that are scrutinized. But our experience of the organic, sun-ripened tomato offers us completely different evidence. In terms of taste and smell, it qualitatively far surpasses the other, and it is both pleasant to eat and nourishing.

For this reason, we cannot exclude experientially derived evidence and expect to successfully represent the entirety of a phenomenon. Through the exclusive consideration of the obvious properties of the two tomatoes, the qualitative dimension is completely overlooked. But the distinction between the two is enormously significant. The one is insipid while the other is delightfully nutritious. The authentic identity of the tomatoes, therefore, resides as strongly with the quality as with the physical appearance.

The feeling-sentient nature of the human being is obviously and necessarily subjective. Consequently, we assume that its evaluation is of less significance than the conclusions of a scientifically driven intellect whose information is physically verifiable. We imagine that reason represents our highest cognitive capacity. But through its oblique and remote functioning and its penchant for quantifiable evidence, we find ourselves preoccupied with the tangible properties of things to the disregard of the qualitative dimension. Furthermore, the materialistic exclusivity is compounded because we assume that the qualitative value of phenomena is only subjectively accessible and of uncertain merit. Therefore, it is marginalized by a prejudicial philosophy.

This predisposed cognitive convention has become progressively more insidious with the advent of technical sophistication. The quantifiable aspects of physical properties can be currently represented with extraordinary precision. Consequently, through excessive confidence in the ingenious reapplication of our discoveries towards invention and our subsequent conviction as to the validity of the materialistic approach, we increasingly doubt the practical value and significance of the qualitative proportion of phenomena.

Thus, we have come to regard the human being almost entirely in terms of physicality. Accordingly, the intrinsic, intangible distinction that essentially distinguishes one person from another, cannot be substantiated in the same manner as the physical, and its significance is also marginalized. Thus, the physical condition is over-extended and assumed to comprise the entirety.

Consequently, in the eyes of materialistic, Western philosophy, only spatial individuality is acknowledged while the intangible, individual distinction remains overlooked because its cannot be conventionally corroborated.

This disastrous practice is adversely influential on many levels, but it is particularly severe in terms of our understanding of the human being. Nevertheless, the incorporeal, singular distinction of the individual, that is our authentic identity, remains the essential prerequisite of immediate cognition whereby we discern essential significances. In other words, the experiential recognition of the independent and intrinsic individuality of human being is vital in order to arrive a definitive knowledge both of our own particular, existential circumstances and the substantive constitution of the phenomenal world.

1. THE HUMAN IPSEITY

The essential human being is an intangible entity whose legitimate condition of existence, is scarcely recognizable through our conventional cognitive practices. Consequently, we have established a distorted understanding of ourselves that places the individual within very limited parameters. Predictably, from the same narrow point of view, it is difficult to realistically foresee a successive prospect towards authentic, human liberty.

As it stands, the sole cognitive agency capable of recognizing the quintessence of the human being and the essential significance of other phenomena is the intrinsic, human entity whose very existence is presently disputed. Furthermore, conventional cognition through intellectual assessment and by feeling sentient evaluation, are oblique practices that pale in profundity beside the direct, experiential engagement of the human ipseity.

The human, singular distinction of existence, through the immediacy of the engagement, discovers itself and, subsequently, the substantial, elemental condition of all other phenomena. Therefore, the cognitive practice of direct encounter whereby the authentic identity of the human being straightforwardly confronts a phenomenon, is an original experience of perception.

Immediate cognition is as unlike our conventional approach, as awake is to sleep. It is as if one were to arouse oneself from slumber and discover that one had indeed, been dreaming and be astonished at the deception of the imagery. The dream may seem to have been entirety authentic until we became alert to an altogether more substantial condition of existence, evident upon waking.

This analogy does not suggest that conventional cognition is entirely void of value and significance, but merely that it does not encompass or represent the complete compass of human and phenomenal existence. This is because intellect and feeling assessment offer only a very limited and particular perspective that overemphasizes a physical view of existence, owing to the narrow scope of those practices.

In other words, while it is not entirely valid to claim that the conventional human practice of interpretive cognition through reason and feeling-sentient evaluation, is uninformed, nevertheless, it is justified once the profundity of immediate cognition is discovered. This is because the immediate, experiential cognition of the full dimensionality of existence requires the establishment of the perspective of the essential identity of the human being and experiential awareness of the human ipseity is relatively uncommon.

If the cognitive perspective of the human, essential ipseity is juxtaposed against the corporeal faculties and functions, those operations are found to be without the significance offered by the direct approach. In other words, the distinction between perception through the corporeal capacities and knowledge through immediate engagement reveals an astonishing discrepancy. This is inevitable because the direct engagement of phenomena, from the perspective of our uniquely individual singularity of existence, reveals the condition in which things exist as elementally as the quintessential existence of the observer.

The conventional, cognitive approach also relies upon pre-established intelligence and acumen that, by virtue of its explicative nature, distorts the possibility of original perception, whereby we overlook the existential significance of phenomena. Therefore, we rely upon a variety of interpretive intermediaries that arise either through our characteristic, emotional disposition or our accumulated, intellectual understanding. Consequently, the direct, experiential engagement of both our own singularity and also the intrinsic condition of other phenomena is avoided, and we concern ourselves solely with apparent conditions of our own interpretation.

However, it is not merely the intellectual preoccupation of the individual and the subsequent, explanatory imposition grafted upon phenomena and events, that distorts our recognition of the authentic condition of things, but any preconceived, expository philosophy. Indeed, frequently, even human intellectual assessment is not original but selectively slanted in favor of a particular conviction.

In terms of an authentic knowledge of circumstances, we have somehow arrived at a comprehensive confusion that remains, for the most part, remote from reality. In fact, typically, humanity operates according to contradictory postulates because of the abstract and indirect nature of our perception.

Nevertheless, the authentic condition of existence is unambiguously discovered experientially and directly, through an immediate encounter by the human singularity of existence. That is to say, the ipseity is the human entity itself, and not merely a corporeal function or feeling sentient assessment. Accordingly, the uniquely individual identity of every human being is found to exist essentially and, consequently, through direct cognition, our singular particularity is able to discover the essential condition of all other phenomena.

In summary, the severely confusing evaluation of existence offered by the conventional cognitive approach is inevitably inadequate because it is derived from a shallow and inconsistent view. Further, in terms of existential authenticity, human rationale is unreliable because it is inevitably distorted by predispositional partiality.

However, if we wish to know the authentic identity and value of something, we are less interested in what we surmise and evaluate it to be and we are more significantly concerned with what it is in its own right. Therefore, in order to discover the essential particularity of something, it is necessary that the perspective of observation should be similarly fundamental. Simply put, established as the primary standpoint, from whose point of view all phenomena may be straightforwardly engaged, the individual ipseity is able to discover the inherent existence of things because it engages them essentially without intermediary translation. In other words, the human essence recognizes the similarly elemental condition of other phenomena.

2. STRAIGHTFORWARD COGNITION

The ipseity is the intrinsic identity of the human being. Accordingly, from the essential perspective, we find that the fundamental existence of an entity is entirely incommensurate with the corporeal appearance.

Conventional understanding is ambiguous by virtue of an inconsistent methodology. Indeed, acutely honed and refined as scientific practices appear to be, through the indirect manner of their application they cannot offer an unequivocal understanding of existence.

For example, reason does not directly experience because it is a function without intrinsic distinction. In other words, the intellect is an operation, not a being. Consequently, as a corporeal function, the mental approach inevitably operates implicitly because it is not an entity capable of direct engagement.

Only an entity is capable of immediate cognition. It is commonly supposed by materialistic, Western philosophy, that the identity of the human being is limited to the corporeal appearance. But the body is a vehicle that serves an intrinsic host that alone possesses selfhood.

While it is minimally ceded by the materialist that the tangible condition probably possesses intangible extension, the physically elusive distinction of the individual is not acknowledged to be independent of the body. Thus, the physical alone is deemed to posses ultimate significance.

However, through comparison with our quintessential existence, our corporeal condition is experientially discovered to be a transient, biological organization. But the human ipseity is not defined by the physical appearance, but it is incorporeally established in a condition of continence.

Thus, the ipseity and the physical representation of the human being, are of an entirely dissimilar nature. The former is the entity itself, while the latter is the medium whereby the host may experience corporeal existence. Every human being must discover this for themselves because upon the experiential recognition of the individual, human ipseity rests our capacity to recognize the authentic condition and meaningfulness of all other things.

Certainly, the human body, as a transient organic vehicle is possessed of general but not specific identity, and as such it offers a focus of correspondence between people. But all human bodies are founded upon common principles of construction and function. They differ in appearance through the cumulative influences of the emotional dispositions of our forebears and through the effects of our own demeanors and propensities. But the body is not an entity; it is a common conveyance. The many human bodies essentially remain the same and retain an identical conceptual origin. The human entity, however, possesses unique significance.

The human ipseity possesses the capacity to experience the essential existence of itself, that of others and of the intrinsic condition of phenomena because it is a unique singularity. Immediate engagement from the perspective of our authentic identity is possible because it is directly experiential. For this reason, it is possible to arrive at definitive knowledge concerning the actual state of the existence of phenomena.

Conversely, an organism without a host would function according to the directive of the principles upon which it is established, but it cannot recognize itself because it does not posses a uniquely distinctive existence to discover. In other words, the human body is not an entity and the essential existence of the human being should not be misidentified with its physical functions however heightened these faculties may be.

The error of the philosopher René Descartes (1596 – 1650) lies within the intellectually founded misidentification of the human thinking faculty with essential being. He might have similarly proposed, I feel, therefore, I am, as many other people fancifully maintain. But neither the activities of the intellect nor of the corporeally swayed feeling nature, can identify the singular entity of the human being.

The ipseity must discern its own existence. Indeed, all intangible phenomena can only be definitively known experientially through direct engagement, but faculties cannot accomplish immediate cognition. Their significance remains beyond the reach of reason except through the implication of circumstantial evidence. But the intellect as a faculty is incapable of experiential engagement and must necessarily operate obliquely because it is without intrinsic identity.

To clarify, the intrinsic singularity of a person can directly engage a situation and discover its intangible significance through straightforward encounter, but a corporeal function cannot. In order that the full, existential dimension of a thing may be discovered, an experiential encounter must occur through the condition of immediacy. In other words, the nature of the existence of something can be known definitively, only if it is engaged without an intermediary. Alternatively, neither can the intellect conclusively evaluate the authenticity of something that is otherwise intangible, for the same reason: thought is incapable of direct experience.

The intellect works with information and evaluates, but without the capability of an immediate encounter it cannot definitely acknowledge the significance of intangible values and elemental existence because they exist in an intellectually unapproachable condition. That is to say, the intellect works at the service of the human being as an indirect processor, but it is not the master.

Similarly, human feeling-sentience may instinctively intuit the impalpable value of something but through its subjective predisposition, it can never decisively identify incorporeal significances. Accordingly, an immediate encounter by the human ipseity is the ultimate cognitive capacity of the human being because the human essence is a singular entity that exists in an essential condition wherein all things are immediately and experientially encountered.

At the present time, there exists a tension between the conclusions of the intellect and the unverifiable convictions of the human, feeling-sentient nature. The well-functioning intellect presents an interpretative schematic that is established almost exclusively upon that which can be tangibly justified. This is because, only the tangible can be conclusively proven to exist and further, logically processed by the intellect. In other words, the intellect deals most successfully with demonstrable fact.

Conversely, intangible value is experienced by every human being even though human sentiment is notoriously fickle. Consequently, the testimony of suspicion and presentiment remains of dubious merit because emotional convictions remain beyond the capability of the intellect to justify. Therefore, convictions, founded upon feeling-sentience offer only an imperfect representation of existence. Thus, while our feeling nature knows of intangible values and impalpable significances, it cannot conclusively identify the significant from subliminal preoccupation.

Similarly, abstract rationale is able to calculate and logically originate a reasonable, intellectual picture of existence, but inevitably it will be founded almost exclusively upon the most blatant physical evidence. However, theoretically, human feeling-sentience and the intellect together offer a modicum of balance to the exclusively cerebral perspective, but in fact, the intellect has philosophically taken precedence over feeling-sentience.

In summary, the intrinsic significance of phenomena is necessarily experienced directly, but not through our human, feeling-sentience. Only the little recognized, singular identity of the human being possesses the inherent facility of immediate cognition because it exists substantively. This is because it exists within an intangible condition wherein the intrinsic state of things is imminently and experientially extant.

With this in mind, we cannot continue to regard existence superficially and imagine that obvious, physical appearances comprise the entirety of existence. Therefore, it would behoove us to set aside the prejudicial stance and with all seriousness investigate the practice of immediate cognition because the shallow view offers a woefully insufficient ideology.

Consequently, the conventionally entertained, predetermined position towards existence offered by materialism and supported by colossal intelligence, will be found to be excruciatingly narrow. This is inevitable because only the existence of the tangible is logically and irrefutably demonstrable through scientific discipline.

Therefore, unable to directly experience

phenomena itself, reason determines the nature of things obliquely, through information gleaned systematically from the physical appearance of things. But, in order to discover the full dimension of existence, the immediate encounter of the human ipseity of existence is essential because definitive, existential knowledge remains beyond the capability and reach of both reason and feeling-sentience.

3. INTRINSIC VALUE

Conventionally, we perceive phenomena only superficially, convinced of the exclusive significance of the material appearance. It appears that the human being does not possess any comparative, cognitional expedient but must scrutinize the physical and endeavor to understand its greater relevance. Nevertheless, a retreat into speculation and superstition is an anathema to the modern mind. Consequently, we strive to become increasingly more skillful and sophisticated in our phenomenal analysis in order to compensate for the obvious deficiency of the conventional, materialistic approach.

However, remaining almost, solely preoccupied with the tangible appearance of things we suspect that the most conspicuous view offers only a very shallow and cursory understanding. Indeed, through an exclusive emphasis on the self-evident, we imagine ourselves in an existence of astonishing complexity. It seems to function automatically under impersonal physical law that is without inaugural influence, but, nevertheless, mindless and miraculous at the same time.

Furthermore, our studies teach us that organic life possesses an astonishing capacity of reproduction and of form rectification, but again we attribute species propagation and form modification to caprice because we find no viable evidence to the contrary. Consequently, either things are as curious as they seem or we have somehow overlooked a more profound and critical interpretation.

The difficulty with an exclusively, physically founded understanding of life is that it discriminates against and overlooks the significance of the qualitative dimension of phenomena. If we cannot explicitly measure and calibrate the quality and intrinsic significance of something, inevitably our comprehension will remain focused upon plainly apparent evidence. But material conditions are not the entirety. Everything possesses substantive significance that can be directly experience but cannot be successfully, physically represented. We may fleetingly acknowledge the qualitative dimension of something and admit to its existence, but, nevertheless, fail to recognize that the intangible value of something represents the intrinsic significance. Consequently, if we disregard the constitutional character of phenomenal expression, only the carapace of the event remains to be studied.

Fore example, when we consider the avian kingdom from the perspective of conventional arrangements, we find that different birds are arranged according to the commonalities of their physical appearance. With painstaking detail creatures are grouped and classified in conformity with certain generalities that define all birds as avians.

However, If we compare the qualitative

distinctions of different species, we become aware that we quickly veer away from the obvious, physical generalities or discrepancies, and recognize the intangible value that distinguishes the characteristic nature of one variety of bird from another. Indeed, the same expressive value is represented through every detail of the creature. In other words, the qualitative difference between the beak of the hawk and that of the dove reveal the intrinsic differences between them.

Furthermore, when the entire bird form is considered from a qualitative perspective, it is found that every aspect and particular conforms to an intangible, intrinsic distinction that characterizes the quality whereby the particular avian expression is physically embodied.

The qualitative distinction of a creature is the manner whereby the commonalities that, for example, epitomize the avian, are specifically exemplified. Seen from this perspective, it is readily evident that the same archetypal commonalities are unconditionally supported, but according to a characteristic motif that epitomizes the intrinsic nature of the species.

The cruel hook of the hawk's beak, the violent scream, the piercing eye and lacerating talon, epitomize the particular, qualitative distinction of the animal, which is morphologically reechoed throughout every minutia of its appearance and further revealed in its temperament.

That is to say, the intangible, qualitative designation of a creature is revealed through the entirety of a very specific form-expression that epitomizes the prevailing nature. Thus, it is the cumulative, inherent predisposition that determines the tonal character and subsequent depiction of the explicit form.

Meanwhile, the gentle mourning dove coos plaintively from the leafy branches. Its bill is only slightly bowed and the body is rounded and soft. Furthermore, the velvety appearance is thoroughly represented by a benign character. Everywhere, the symbol of peace and gentleness, the dove is the avian expression of mildness and passivity.

Clearly, the qualitative motif of the physical appearance of a creature disguises a more profound reality that is discovered through immediate consideration to be of enormous, morphological significance. But this cannot be recognized through the analysis of the physical minutiae but it is discerned from the metaphorical declaration that typifies the totality.

Direct cognition requires the maintenance of an essential connection between the observer and the object of interest. Consequently, we avoid the inclination to extrapolate and conjecture concerning evidence that is gleaned from the peripheral details. The mechanical activity, chemical composition and electrical properties of an organism, for example, do not reveal what a creature is but merely some aspects of the functioning. For example, the intrinsic identity of the hawk or the mourning dove remains inaccessible to physical analysis because the qualitative distinction that essentially differentiates the intrinsic disposition of one animal from another exists intangibly.

If we examine a collection of different bird eggs, we find that each shell is particularly distinct and exemplifies the qualitative identity of the specific avian in egg form. Every egg is of a certain character that exemplifies the essential identity of the creature. In a broader sense, no aspect or detail of a bird can exist independently of the particular, qualitative distinction of the entirety.

Qualitative distinction exists intangibly as the intrinsic identifier of a creature. It is the essential nomen that differentiates one creature from another because it describes the characteristic impetus or expression that is the incentive of a specific form. Consequently, it is of far greater significance to explore the qualitative distinctions and inherent differences of character between creatures that to attempt to distinguish them through an abstract analysis of deoxyribonucleic acid.

The qualitative differentiation is the manner whereby the general avian concept is particularly realized. However, an exclusive preoccupation with the physical appearance fails to reveal the qualitative motif of expression that defines the entire animal. Consequently, conventional typology is misleading if it does not reveal the intrinsic dynamic towards organic diversity based upon qualitative criteria.

Intangibles are only recognized experientially and cannot be accredited in the same manner as physically derived evidence. It is imperative that the significance of intangible value be recognized and explored because everything possesses qualitative merit that reveals its inherent distinction and identity.

Nevertheless, we prefer to rely on physically pertinent information and intelligence, but in reality, the physical appearances of phenomena do not represent the entirety. If we dismiss the qualitative dimension of existence because it is intangible and assumes it to be a mere adjunct of the corporeal without particular importance, then we find ourselves restricted to a narrow superficial perspective, physically precise but void of essential meaning.

It is the qualitative distinction of existence of a phenomenon that reveals the significance and particular identity. That is to say, the intrinsic identity does not originate in the physical appearance but exists intangibly. But the nature of the existence of a particular phenomenon is discovered through experiential engagement because characteristic timbre is discernible through receptive attention.

In terms of biology, while creatures and plants may be generally classified as aeriform, arboreal, terrestrial, subterranean or aquatic, these conditions are not conventionally recognized as qualitative propensities. Nevertheless, the characteristic predisposition of a creature may be further distinguished through the cumulative consolidation of persistent qualitative tendencies over myriad generations. In other words, the manner whereby animal nature is particularly expressed under varying ecological circumstances, is represented through form differentiation that accrues as the foundation of subsequent, idiosyncratic response and adaption towards changing circumstances.

Inherent distinction is discerned when the human ipseity immediately engages a phenomenon and inquires in what qualitative manner the one creature distinguishes itself and differs essentially from another. The subsequent realization of the differences of demeanor and disposition between creatures becomes blatantly obvious from the moment that the qualitative dimension of a creature is recognized as the distinguishing factor between animals.

In other words, the inherent identity of phenomena lies less in the physical appearance and more significantly with the intangible distinction. That distinction rests upon the qualitative condition of the existence of a thing which is not found merely in the physical semblance.

Presently, our perspective towards life is severely constrained because we rely almost exclusively upon the evidence of material conditions. Our subsequent understanding remains narrow because it is founded upon the physical analysis of what can only be described as a veneer or facade.

For example, the intangible, qualitative distinction between otherwise similar phenomena, such as Native Element Minerals, colors or organic forms, epitomizes the inherent identity. The physical properties of something do not intrinsically identify it, but they only describe the material condition. In other words, the appearance of a thing alone offers insufficient evidence of its intrinsic existence because the material condition superimposes the intangible, essential meaning and significance.

It is difficult for us to grasp that phenomena are not exclusively represented by their appearances because we have become familiar with a unidimensional, materialistic perspective. Yet, we engage the qualitative proportion of existence all the time, although we have minimized its significance in preference for the easily justifiable, physical circumstances.

The intangible significance of phenomena becomes evident through the immediate engagement of the human ipseity as the essential, cognitive perspective of the human being. But the intellect functions logically and systematically endeavoring to simulate mathematical precision, which is the ideal manner of its operation. However, the intellect cannot attain the same conclusive proof through logic and sequential rationale, that it ideally achieves through calculation. Nevertheless, we endeavor, as far as possible, to reduce information concerning phenomena into quantifiable terms. Yet, we find that it is not possible to render qualitative values in this manner because they exist intangibly and cannot be measured and calibrated in the manner of physical circumstances. Thus, we marginalize the significance and merit of the qualitative value of things and elevate the superficial appearance assuming that the entirety is satisfactorily represented.

Today, we rely almost exclusively upon physical evidence and, through exhaustive analysis, we reduce and strive to quantify every detail in order to approach a mathematical semblance of a phenomenon for the convenience of the human intellect. Furthermore, we estrange ourselves from a fuller appreciation of the significance of the qualitative dimension of existence through the establishment of abstract, philosophical constructions instead of directly engaging the phenomena themselves.

If we insist that the physical appearance of something represents its entirety, we must somehow explain phenomena exclusively in terms of material evidence. Naturally, the superficial characterization that is commonly accepted is the inevitable consequence.

Yet, experientially, we know that the appearance does not constitute the entirety and, consequently, we must apply ourselves diligently in an effort to satisfactorily explain the discrepancy. However, to establish hypothetical expositions whereby we try to envisage possible philosophical justifications for the condition of things is devious. The suppositional approach works well with physically derived knowledge because it leads to invention. But, in terms of understanding the human condition, a theory possess no existential reality but remains an abstract construct without existential value until proven.

Abstract conjecture cannot achieve existential knowledge concerning something because the intangible significance of a thing is only discovered experientially. A significant dimension of its existence is overlooked and, consequently, we strive to discover what something is, based upon partial evidence. One may imagine that the abstract construct has merit but unless it is founded upon the entirety of a phenomenon it inevitably conflicts with reality. Required is a practice of cognition that allows us to discover the complete significance of phenomena including the conveniently ignored, intangible dimension of their existence.

4. INTRINSIC EXISTENCE

Although it is readily possible to experientially discover the intangible, qualitative significance of something, without the aegis of the human ipseity, the results will be, inevitably, subjectively influenced. This is because the conventional faculty whereby we recognize the impalpable, is our capricious, feeling nature. However, the singular significance of our existence engages the essential value of phenomena immediately, without subjective or intellectual evaluation. We do not conceptualize or interpret a phenomenon but encounter it purposefully and directly from the condition of our unique existence.

It is the direct nature of the encounter between the human, essential identity and the phenomenon that is of significance. The corporeally established faculties of reason and conjecture are restrained from assuming prior knowledge, and human feeling-sentience is not permitted to distort the candid engagement between the human essential identity and the phenomenon. In this manner, the encounter occurs without intermediary translation and bias but arises when something is originally experienced by the human, individual distinction of existence.

The unalloyed engagement between the human, individual distinction and a phenomenon is necessarily experiential because the conventional faculties of cognition that involve rationale and logic, are intentionally inhibited. Thereby, a condition of cognitive directness is established between the human, individual distinction and the object of attention. By this means, both the physical and qualitative conditions of phenomenal existence are recognized and we discover the full-dimensionality of things. The physical serves to anchor and focus our interest, whereby, the ipseity discerns the essential significance.

For example, we recognize the qualitative distinction between two different trees through an examination of their lumber. We overlook the visible properties of the wood and endeavor to discover in what manner the two samples differ qualitatively from one another.

In order to express the qualitative differentiation, however, we cannot use the vernacular that is appropriate to describe the physical aspects because qualities and values do not possess tangible existence of themselves, and they cannot be materially isolated and described.

In other words, the intangible significance of something can only be discerned directly and experientially because, without physical representation, our conventional cognitive faculties cannot assimilate incorporeal evidence. Therefore, in order to ensure that knowledge concerning the intangible value of something is not merely imaginatively derived, it must be experienced by the human, essential identity.

The human, essential identity serves as the ultimate benchmark of reality because it exists as the individual distinction and possesses original significance. That is to say, within the human constitution, there is nothing as authentic as the unique, individual distinction. Therefore, from the perspective of the human ipseity, the essential singularity of others is readily discerned, and the intangible dimension of phenomena becomes evident.

Intangibles must be experienced in order to be recognized and, in order to conclusively identify the authentic condition of existence of something, the human essence itself must directly engage the phenomenon. The human essence experientially recognizes itself, and subsequently, the unique and incorporeal significance of others and the intangible existence of phenomena. This is possible because the human, individual distinction exists intangibly just as the qualitative significances that differentiate phenomena occur intrinsically. However, the human ipseity cannot be physically described except perhaps metaphorically through the medium of fine art because in its material condition it is only represented superficially.

We portray intangible significances, such as qualities and values, figuratively and metaphorically because they exist essentially and must be similarly described. As intangibles, they cannot be successfully articulated through physical criteria because they are neither measurable nor calculable, but unidimensional.

Or, to put it another way, they exist immanently.

Consequently, the appropriate way to portray a quality that is without a physical significance, is through qualitative representation. But first we must directly engage the phenomenon itself through immediate cognition in order to discern the intrinsic distinction. However, it is critical that the human, feeling-sentient nature be restrained because, otherwise, we merely determine how we feel concerning something, and not how it exists in its own right.

As an aside, we notice strong subjectivity in much modern art that may be of interest to the psychologist but remains moot in terms of the essential description of intrinsic realities. In other words, a subjective interpretation merely indicates our own response towards a condition. It does not definitively reveal the authentic nature of the phenomenon as it exists, of itself.

The human intangible distinction of existence is the individual ipseity that differentiates and discerns between essential circumstances. It is the incorporeal significance of the human being that is not represented physically. However, from the perspective of the ipseity, a phenomenon is immediately experienced, and its essential, intangible condition of existence becomes known. It is the same incorporeal value that the fine artist wishes to articulate and strives to do so through a mastery of the language of a particular artistic medium.

But the artist's feeling-sentient interpretation of

something is irrelevant when it comes to revealing the authentic condition of its existence. However, the moment that we set aside out feeling-sentience and resist interpreting the qualitative value of something from our own idiosyncratic perspective, something unexpected occurs. Restraining conventional cognition and established practices of intellectual appraisal and sentimental estimation, we discover an entire volume of intrinsic significance that is far more meaningful than the appearance. Indeed, it qualifies the physical with substantive connotations.

For example, when we attempt to discover the qualitative distinction between two different species of wood irrespective of our pre-conceptions and presumptions concerning them, immediately, our own authentic and incorporeal existence establishes itself as our point-of-view. That is to say, when conventional cognition is restrained, the ipseity inevitably becomes established as our point of view. Thereby, the intrinsic particularity that epitomizes the phenomena becomes discernible.

Consequently, we can see that it is unnecessary to embark upon an exhaustive training whereby we establish the ipseity as the individual seat of consciousness. We merely constrain the noisy mind, whereby, the perspective of the ipseity becomes the principle viewpoint.

This occurs because the approach whereby the

human quintessence engages phenomena is immediate, without any interpretative impediment. The ipseity resides within the same condition of immediacy with the intrinsic condition of all other phenomena. It is through the aegis of this concurrence that we are able to directly encounter the inherent significance of each of the wood samples and discover in what manner they are intrinsically and qualitatively distinguished.

Unprejudiced by evaluation and estimation, phenomena are found as they exist elementally. Furthermore, through immediate cognition, we discover that the fundamental circumstances and identity of things exist not spatially but immediately. Therefore, when we engage a phenomenon from the point-of-view of our own incorporeal existence, we discover the way things are intrinsically as opposed to peripherally. Clearly, there exist two existential magnitudes accessible to the human mind. The spatial material proportion is the peripheral carapace while the essential volume exists immanently and encompasses the intrinsic, meaningful significance of things.

Immanent significance qualifies the material appearance with substantive connotations. The physical appears senseless without substantive connotation because it is perceived without intrinsic qualification. It is for this reason, that many balk at the presumption of materialistic, Western philosophy because it contradicts their own direct experience. However, through immediate engagement and the restraint of presumptive evaluation, we directly discern the significant essence of phenomena and their qualitative merit.

The fine artist endeavors to portray the original, elemental existence of a thing without reservation. Or, in the same way that we meet other individuals and discover the essential significance of their particular existence, the artist strives to represent the essential reality.

When we discover the unique existence of someone else, from the perspective of our own essence and determine that they are similarly graced, it validates our own self-recognition. It is through self-reflection that we discover our essential existence and from the perspective of our authentic identity, we establish through practical application, the value of immediate cognition. But we find that through direct engagement we can also determine, similarly essential identities.

Furthermore, if we recognize the intrinsic existence of others and the inherent significance of phenomena, then it sanctions the authenticity of our own ipseity because immediate cognition is only possible through the perspective of the incorporeal, singularity of our existence. In other words, our original and singular existence is discovered to reside in an intangible condition wherein all phenomena exist immediately.

Formerly in earlier times, human cognition was indirect and evaluative. However, gradually we found that the subjective stance towards life offered only an unreliable foundational basis and we increasingly developed and now rely upon reason as the arbiter of authenticity.

Notwithstanding, through the indirect nature and functioning of the intellect, definitive knowledge remained remote unless we could somehow reduce experiences into a quantifiable condition whereby the intellect could calculate with a precision, alike to mathematical proof, and discover conclusive justification.

Unfortunately, the resultant, philosophical structure resembles the source from which quantifiable intelligence is most readily derived and we find that we have established a perspective towards life founded exclusively upon physical evidence. This erroneous position has confined and restrained us within a mentality that is apparently reasonable but essentially, unreal. Thus, we find ourselves in a state of existential bondage because we have established our outlook towards life upon a discriminatory exclusivity of physical evidence that, in reality, suggests a condition that does not exist.

While human, feeling-sentience offers only subjective evaluation, sanctioning a cognitive monopoly founded almost exclusively upon physical evidence, is equally erroneous. Fortunately, the individual, singular significance of existence allows us to engage phenomena directly and through that immediate cognitive encounter we discover the full volume of existence. Thereby, we recognize that the incorporeal significances of things are more pertinent than the physical in terms of intrinsic significance, and that comparatively, exclusive materialism is no more than a humanly contrived excess.

5. HUMAN INCORPOREAL EXISTENCE

Scholarship and technical acumen are not of direct service in the practice of immediate cognition. However, the discipline of systematic inquiry and the determination not to be distracted by emotional hyperbole and general consensus in an invaluable preparation.

We are justifiably dissatisfied with convictions founded merely upon enthusiasm or agile rhetoric in both popular scientific circles and the religious assembly. It is disappointing to be assured of the significant importance of an approach towards life only to find it inconsequential. Considering that our purpose is to discover the authentic nature of existence, we must disentangle the superficial and irrelevant from the significant in order to move forward.

Significant progress is attainable exclusively through understanding what is really going on and immediate cognition allows us to discern the elemental condition of things. However, the direct, cognitive approach is properly founded upon the perspective of our intrinsic singularity because the only thing that a human being really possesses is the reality of individual existence. Consequently, the intrinsic, human distinction discerns the similarly essential significance of all other phenomena.

The human ipseity is clearly not a transient, physical thing nor is it a faculty of our corporeal condition. Consequently, when a phenomenon is confronted from the most profound perspective of all, a dynamic of immediate engagement occurs wherein we experience the object intrinsically and discern its fundamental significance of existence.

Immediate cognition requires the restraint of the conventional, evaluative activities and the moderation of feeling-sensibility. Thereupon, the human ipseity becomes appropriately positioned as the sovereign perspective from which to engage all circumstances. Consequently, from the essential perspective we discover that the intrinsic conditions both of the observer and of the object, exist timelessly.

In other words, through immediate cognition, we find that the intrinsic significance of physical phenomena exists in a condition beyond the influence of time and magnitude. Therein, the substantive volume of things exists in immanent relationship with one another, distinguishable through the particular, qualitative differentiation that epitomizes their existence.

In the manner whereby we directly discern the most profound distinction that qualifies a physical object with significance, similarly, we discover our own incorporeal condition through experiential engagement. Once the human quintessence is successfully recognized, the inherent, intangible existence of all other things is readily encountered through immediate cognition from the point-of-view of our incorporeal permanence.

Nevertheless, we do not like to restrain reason because we are well aware of the value of rationale and systematic deduction. Furthermore, it is commonly imagined that the sole alternative to intellectual appraisal is some kind of mystical experience without sensible foundation or realism. Indeed, it may well be that the opposite proposition other than deduction is only empirically unfounded belief, unsubstantiated conviction or faith, and we find ourselves no better off than before.

If this were so, we would have to concede that the capability of achieving definite, existential knowledge lies beyond the reach of human cognition. We would have to content ourselves with a meager, materialistic philosophy or align ourselves with an agreeable belief system that purports to possess an otherwise unattainable, comprehensive knowledge concerning existence.

Consequently, it is necessary to understand what immediate engagement really is through personal research. Thereby, quieting the thinking and feeling, the perspective of the human, incorporeal existence necessarily takes precedent.

What we are trying to discover through firsthand inquiry is the efficacy of the immediate approach whereby we permit the object of our interest to be recognized upon the basis of the characteristic timbre of the intrinsic nature. But only the human, essential ipseity can discern intrinsic conditions, consequently the conventional cognitive functions must be suspended.

In the same vein, anticipating the protest that immediate cognition is merely subjective appraisal, we also suspend the intrusion of instinctual and visceral evaluation and maintain an entirely clear mind. Thereupon, there occurs a pristine engagement as if it were the very first occasion that we set eyes upon the object, and through insight we discover the intrinsic nature of existence.

Similarly, the same approach anticipates the recognition of our own singular distinction. In other words, once more, the mind is quieted in order to allow an uncorrupted view whereupon the human, essential ipseity directly experiences its own uniqueness.

The cognitive engagement between the human, authentic condition of existence and a phenomenon, through impartial discernment, requires an open mind. The quieting of the mind and the emotions means precisely that. The quiddity discovers essential things only because it resides substantively. If we imagine that an exploration of the dynamic of immediate cognition, merely requires superficial attention and lackadaisical application, we vastly underestimate the significance of this discussion.

The consequence of the development of the human capacity of immediate cognition through the aegis of the human, incorporeal quintessence, alludes to the possibility of cognitive autonomy. We discover through the direct experience of our singular existence, the authentic condition of all other things. Recognizing the inherent identity, intrinsic significance and qualitative importance of phenomena presents a multidimensional perspective towards existence that is both physically established and incorporeally substantive. Indeed, this is the way things exist in reality.

Immediately engaging essential conditions, we find that we enter an immanent status wherein everything resides authentically. Thus, we recognize the error of an exclusively materialistic perspective whereby we occupy ourselves merely with appearances and perceive only the most obvious relevance of phenomena. Thereby, the intrinsic significance of things is marginalized because it exists nonphysically. But the remainder is a very shallow perspective entirely without meaningful consequence.

The unrecognized intrinsic value of things and the qualitative nature holds profound existential significance. If we deal solely with corporeally derived evidence at the expense of the intangible merit, the ensuing philosophy will be similarly superficial.

Established as the principal, cognitive perspective, our singular identity engages all things imminently, encountering them elementally. Thereby, the human ipseity is found to occupy a condition of permanency and immediacy, without physical dimension. It rests assuredly in the reality of its existence and from that position it engages all things straightforwardly, and through direct experience discovers the similarly essential distinction of existence of all phenomena.

Therefore, the value of the physical appearance of a thing is dependent upon its intangible impetus. In other words, the inherent condition of the existence of things, reveals the authentic identity, while the transient, palpable substance represents the consequence. Indeed, we are soon dissatisfied with the superficial semblance when once we discover that we exist profoundly in a far more meaningful condition, and we learn to differentiate between existential significances.

The information that we derive through an exhaustive scrutiny of the material appearance of things and an investigation of their physical properties, is found to be existentially of marginal significance. Nevertheless, we pile more and more physically derived evidence on top of former scholarship and thereby hope to discover the substance of things as if essentials existed materially.

Vainly, we try to discover existential meaning through an examination of the effect, while significance is inherent alone to the origin, which is the existential condition in which the human, incorporeal singularity resides. Imagining that the more information that we accrue concerning the nature of the physicality of phenomena can somehow reveal the intrinsic significance of things is the typical stance of materialistic, Western philosophy.

However, the peripheral condition of something

does not posses the same substance as the origin but it only represents the carapace. In other words, the significance of things is not found in their corporeal circumstances but within their intangible merit and distinction. We discover the existential relevance of something when we cease to be preoccupied with the physical appearance and directly engage the essential condition from the perspective of our own singular distinction of existence.

6. SUBSTANTIVE SIGNIFICANCE

Concerning the phenomenal world, we may ask ourselves how things function and imagine from the workings that we will discover what something is. Thereby, we confuse function with identity. Often, when we pose the question how, our inquiries lead us to the appropriate conclusions concerning the mechanics of things. Furthermore, in a more profound way, we approach life philosophically with the question why and yet again we probably envisage that the apparent, practical purpose of something explains its existence.

This occurs because, increasingly, we have come to regard existence in physical and mechanical terms. Indeed, materialistic Western philosophy is basically founded upon lifeless principles.

The how question should address the workings of a phenomenon, and the why pertains to its intentionality. Nevertheless, the modern materialistic approach exhaustively scrutinizes and analyzes something, and thereby we endeavor to comprehend phenomenal existence through an understanding of the functionality. Furthermore, we extrapolate a philosophy explaining life based upon operations.

The application and relevance of something also do not explain its existence but we assume that our superficial discoveries reveal everything there is to know regarding the identity of a phenomenon.

In reality, neither how nor why, approach the intrinsic identity of a thing. In order to determine the existential significance of something we must ask ourselves the question what. That question addresses the profound, inherent constitution of the phenomenon, as it is, irrespective of function and application.

In other words, the question what is not answered through an understanding of mechanical, chemical or electrical processes. Neither is it addressed by a consideration of its purpose. Consequently, a materialistically established philosophy cannot answer existential questions because the issue of what something is concerns the intrinsic significance.

If we discover what something is then its workings and purpose make perfect sense because they are an extension of an existential expression. Nevertheless, ignorance concerning the intrinsic significance of something is not alleviated through an understanding of the way it works or its ostensible intention.

An examination of the how and why, of a thing do not allude to the intrinsic identity of a phenomenon because these questions only allow us to address the physical condition of something. Similarly, speculation as to the use of something, founded exclusively upon tangible evidence, cannot gainsay its intrinsic significance. In other words, the seeming purpose of something, based upon information concerning its superficial appearance, does not approach its authentic identity.

The existential significance of a thing is not the same as its function nor is the assumed purpose based upon the manner of its operation. Both directly concern the material appearance and overlook the existential condition of the phenomenon. Thus, the hierarchy of the material world, physical conditions and mechanical workings belie the intrinsic significance of phenomena.

Similarly, another human being is encountered, and we pose the same question concerning identity if we wish to discover the essential significance that belies the corporeal appearance. But, of course, if we wish to discover the identity of someone else we must rephrase the question to, who are you, not corporeally but intrinsically. Thereby, we recognize the singular condition of existence of the other person and encounter the unique person.

Moreover, we find that we ascertain intrinsic significances through the aegis of our own singular existence. Consequently, the identification of the fundamental identity of something cannot be found through an examination of the working, nor through subsequent speculation concerning purpose, because the distinction of a thing, that identifies what it is, exists intangibly. As such, the particular identity of a thing must be experienced in order to be discovered.

In addition, the how and the why require the application of corporeal faculties that are unable to directly engage phenomena because they are functions and not entities, and they are, consequently, unable to experience things directly. But in order to discover what the fundamental identity of something is, our own intrinsic singularity must engage the phenomenon experientially and immediately.

Engaged directly, the intangible inherence of something is recognized as being of paramount significance because the condition of its existence is synonymous with its innate distinction. The human, incorporeal singularity, for example, is not discovered through an examination of the manner in which the body functions and operates. Nor do we find our essential significance through speculation concerning why the human being exists. But we recognize the quintessential identity of a thing through immediate, cognitive engagement.

The human, intrinsic identity engages all things straightforwardly and, consequently, directly experiences the elementary condition of their existence. However, the reason for the confinement of human cognition to the intellect and our feeling-sentient nature is the misidentification of the human, substantive existence with the body and its functions.

For example, the word spirit is increasingly interchangeable with mind or soul. Similarly, from the material perspective, more and more, the essential person is assumed to be dubiously synonymous with the brain. Consequently, everything is reduced in significance, and the soul is imagined to be a combination of temperament and emotion. Ofttimes, the intrinsic person is suspected of be equivalent with human, nervous system or it is purported to exist as a consequence of our chemical composition. Thus, the human singularity of existence, in some unspecified way, is traced to an electrical impulse or to the biochemical condition of the body.

While intangible experiences such as joy, excitement or intuition do indeed provoke a biochemical consequence and may be discernible as an electrical anomaly within the nervous system, the identity of the human being does not reside within the workings of the corporeal condition. The body responds to the state of the soul. Nevertheless, it is true that the induction of chemical imbalance or the application of electrical stimulus most certainly modifies the equilibrium of our physical constitution and provokes all manner of response particularly to our corporeally influenced feeling-sentience, but the intrinsic distinction of human existence is not consequent upon our bodily condition.

Through oblique cognition, we may imagine that we achieve a measure of autonomy when we abstractly pursue a logical sequence of propositions and hypotheses and satisfy ourselves through rationale of the validity of our conclusions. We systematically scrutinize physically dependent data that we determine to be authentic through its blatancy and assume that we may discover thereby the entire significance of something.

Yet, all our information, in order to be deemed acceptable, must be derived from phenomenal circumstances that can be physically measured and calculated and, consequently, scientifically justified. Thus, through logical sequence that distantly resembles mathematics, we assume that we derive a conclusion that is objectively sound. But through the inequitable scrutiny of data, exclusively derived from concrete conditions, we cannot possible achieve definitive existential knowledge.

In other words, however efficiently we may organize the data, our information is consistently of a physical caliber and, consequently, it remains incomplete because corporeal evidence merely comprises the most obvious dimension of existence. Therefore, if we assume that our singularity of existence is confined to our corporeal constitution then, inevitably, we find ourselves cognitively restricted within the limited scope of our physical capacities. Consequently, we construct a shallow and arid interpretation of life based upon the periphery of things.

Immediate cognition necessitates the establishment of the human, incorporeal singularity as the fundamental mainstay and perspective from where our own intrinsic significance and that of all other phenomena, may be instantly recognized for their existential authenticity. If we deny our incorporeal existence then we can scarcely expect to engage phenomena from a position of independence.

Thus, the direct, experiential recognition of the authentic, singular existence of the human being, is the indispensable requirement of autonomous cognition. Consequently, the elemental condition of something represents the original and extant circumstance that identifies it intrinsically.

While the outward appearance proceeds transiently, the elemental condition exists in a state of consistency. Therefore, the intimate experience of one's elemental existence involves the discovery of the volume in which the essence of things resides fundamentally and permanently. Thereby, the material circumstances anchor our attention, but the essential is the meaningful condition that we discover through the direct experience of the essential selfhood.

7. PREJUDICED CONVICTION

While the unbiased reader may recognize the value of some aspects of this account, the content will remain merely academic unless it is independently explored. The closed-minded individual predisposed to a familiar perspective and loyally determines to maintain an accustomed approach, will merely react defensively. It is pointless to endeavor to persuade the short-sighted because a prejudicial position prevents the necessary disposition, prerequisite to impartial research. If we are convinced of the infallibility of a chosen cognitive approach towards existence then our preconceived practice remains our sole resource.

It is extraordinary how convincing a theoretical interpretation of life can become, even though it did not originate with ourselves. We are persuaded by systematic rhetoric and dialectic, and disposed through consensus to adopt the position of an apparent authority even in the face of our own research and experience. This is because materialistic, Western philosophy has become the entrenched perspective even of the purportedly spiritual devotee, whose rhetoric appears other-worldly but often combines the theoretical conviction of an elusive, ethereal realm with materialism.

The adoption of a seemingly incontestable, abstract interpretation of existence, is particularly obstructive in the light of considerable, supportive scholarship. It is probably imagined that a different perspective towards life threatens their academic achievement. In fact, in terms of existential conditions, erudition is irrelevant because we are not contesting someones ostensible knowledge but we are suggesting an entirely dissimilar cognitive approach that does not involve our intellectual faculties.

It may be that some readers will relate to certain particular factors and that the concept of immediate cognition will, consequently, appeal to them. But if direct experience through the intrinsic, human singularity is imagined to be merely a concept then the reader will have missed the point entirely.

We are not trying to introduce a new abstract construct or a formulaic arrangement but to present a juxtaposition between remote cognition and immediate experience. We misconstrue the intent if we imagine that an imminent engagement of existence is merely an alternative proposition that purports to offer some kind of salvation.

The approach of immediate, experiential engagement through our own essential singularity, is entirely to do with cognition. Pursued with an open mind, many conceptual reversals will be inevitable because conventionally we rely upon a constricted approach that requires indirect summation and intellectual rationale. However, direct cognition involves the immediate engagement of the human ipseity without the distraction of intermediary interpretation and evaluation.

Some of us will already have made some tentative steps towards an experiential recognition of the pivotal dynamic of immediate engagement. Therefore, we recognize that the significance of direct cognition must be individually experienced in order to be qualified because it deals with intangible existence, and the systematic approach of the intellect finds little merit in evidence that cannot be physically justified. Indeed, if a philosophy allowed uncorroborated testimony, we would have to include all manner of fiction and unreason.

Consequently, the intellect has to be selective and systematic in order to manage information, but that is also the shortcoming of reason when it comes to intangible value. It is assumed by materialistic, Western philosophy that the immediate experience of intangible existence is merely a subjective interpretation of physical circumstances. For that reason, material conditions remain the significant certainty of existence and experiential knowledge merely idiosyncratically qualifies it. This position is easily maintained because the authentic identity of the human being is unrecognized as an intangible entity and cognition continues to be indirectly practiced and intellectually evaluated.

Inevitably, that which cannot be physically justified and can only be recognized experientially is incommensurate with the conventional approach. Nevertheless, the human being must experientially discover its authentic identity because our existential significance is incorporeal and, consequently, it can only be pragmatically assessed. This is the reason why the intellectual approach is dissatisfied with intangible, experientially driven knowledge because that is not the manner in which it functions. In other words, the intellect cannot successfully deal with physically unfounded data.

However, the human being is not a corporeal function and, consequently, we possess authority over our reasoning faculties. Through immediate cognition we intentionally suspend our thought processes and our emotional predilection and find that our identity continues, thereby demonstrating that our existence is not synonymous with our intellect because we should otherwise, most certainly, disappear.

But of greater significance is the unfamiliar, cognitive condition that we discover upon restraining our conventional, mental processes. We no longer rely on pre-conceptual determination, abstract conjecture or calculated evaluation but we find ourselves confronting phenomena directly from the perspective of the singular condition of our respective existence.

Furthermore, a brief, experiential examination of our individual uniqueness is sufficient to conclusively assure us that we essentially exist in an autonomous condition. Thus, it is the direct experience of our selfhood that confirms our existential independence. Therefore, it is upon the intrinsic ipseity that the dynamic of direct, experiential cognition rests.

Nevertheless, if this simple act of self-examination is resisted, then the individual remains unhappily fated to remain confined to a very restrictive, cognitive point of view.

Accordingly, the foremost prerequisite of direct cognition is the recognition of the human, unique singularity of existence, through experiential engagement. Thereby, we readily determine that our identity is not contingent upon the body or any of its functions but exists separately and physically unconstrained. Furthermore, repositioning our unique individuality as our principal cognitive perspective, we directly experience phenomena for their intrinsic merit and no longer merely appraise things based upon their superficial properties.

Moreover, we find that other people, similarly, possess a unique originality that is their authentic condition of existence. As a result, we find the physical appearance misleading because it does not reveal who a person is, anymore than the nervous system or any other corporeal interdependency, identifies the intrinsic existence of the human being.

Conventionally, through our limited, cognitive approach to existence, we endeavor to establish a formulaic interpretation of life that we can readily grasp. We imagine that if we establish a comprehensive, explanatory model then everything will become understandable. Consequently, we adhere to an interpretative substitute for existence because it appeals to rational understanding. Nonetheless, in terms of the discovery of the existential significance of things, the abstract construct is recognized as irrelevant and it only hinders the achievement of definitive knowledge that is attainable only through immediate engagement.

Securely established as our cognitive perspective, the human, singular uniqueness experientially engages phenomena and discovers the original condition of their existence. Therefore, that which essentially distinguishes one human identity from another as the particular distinction of singularity, becomes the sovereign identity. Subsequently, we immediately engage phenomena from the perspective of the inherent authority of our unique existence and discover the similarly elemental state in which all other things reside. Thus, we inaugurate an entirely different cognitive approach than the conventional, corporeally established, intellectual perspective or from feeling-sentience, because our authentic identity is able to encounter things directly.

Thus, through direct experience, the human, incorporeal singularity of existence discovers the same elemental condition as the intangible significance of every phenomenal occurrence. When the authentic identity of the human being is recognized through immediate experience, it is discovered that we exist intrinsically and immanently. Hence, we identify the authentic condition of all other phenomena from a most profound perspective.

In retrospect, we wonder how we could have been so consummately mistaken as to our own identity and we recognize the pernicious nature of the deceit. But the moment that we directly experience our intrinsic condition, the misconstrual becomes evident and the entire materialistic, Western philosophical bias is found to be fallacious.

The human, elemental circumstances of existence are intangible but not insubstantial. That is to say, while the physical condition of phenomena displays neither the origin nor the significance of their existence as such, nevertheless, the intrinsic identity of things continue substantively. Thus, the condition of cognitive immediacy involves the recognition of that which is meaningful concerning something which is, otherwise, only perceived superficially.

We know this approach to be acutely applicable to interpersonal relationships, but we fail to realize that it applies similarly to the manner whereby we identify and distinguish other phenomena.

Our significant distinction of existence engages things directly because it exists fundamentally. It does not attempt to obliquely evaluate things because it cannot do so. Indeed, it directly and experientially finds phenomena as they exist essentially, without the necessity of interpretation. Therefore, the dynamic of directness between the human, incorporeal singularity and a situation, occurs immediately in the sense that the essential of all things exist immanently and our perception is similarly straightforward through the profundity of our approach.

For this reason, the immediate experience of the human essential ipseity offers an extraordinary realization that is further compounded upon consistent reapplication. The knowledge that we achieve concerning the existential condition of things is always fundamental and existentially profound because, through the immediacy of our encounter, we experience phenomena as they exist intrinsically. In other words, alike to an artist's rendition, every detail possesses pertinence and meaningfulness. Or analogous to poetry, everything exhibits poignancy because nothing is superfluous and all things are found to possess an inherently relevant significance.

8. TRUE, FALSE - REAL, UNREAL

Essentially, everything is found to possess meaningful significance beyond the physical appearance because the intrinsic relevance of things resides within the intangible condition, as a particular distinction. For example, the unique quality that differentiates one color from another is not successfully described in terms of their physical properties because the intrinsic nature of a color is not revealed in the cursory appearance. Indeed, if we attempt to allocate a physically relevant value to color, we find our numerical representation remote from that of our direct experience. It serves as a representative codification but it cannot replicate the intrinsic significance of the color. In order to do so, we must describe the character of a tone or shade in figurative terms.

Intangible significance is not readily quantifiable and the terminology used to portray the impalpable is, necessarily, of a different caliber from that which is used to describe the material condition of phenomena. Furthermore, the circumstances in which the intangible significance of something resides, is found to be intrinsic as opposed to superficial, by virtue of the definitive manner in which its elemental condition is experientially discovered. Consequently, the intrinsic condition of something is the essential reality because therein resides the significance of a phenomenon.

The values true and false are inappropriately applied to reality because real and unreal are conditions that are more accurately described as real or non-present. From that perspective it is safe to say that only reality exists. Anything other than reality is the consequence of erroneous perception and, consequently, unreality as a condition, is a misnomer. Similarly, true and false cannot refer to actual existence but apply most suitably to mathematical circumstances and, distantly, in terms of logical propositions. Accordingly, when we apply terminology belonging properly to hypothetical and abstract situations, and attempt thereby, to verify a condition of existence, we actually confuse incommensurable language as if it were the same.

A belief or a hypothesis is evaluated upon the strength of the logic of its propositions. But logic cannot determine if a situation is intrinsically real because the authenticity of reality cannot be calculated. Furthermore, logic does not even possess the certainty of mathematics and, consequently, while a position may appear to be true or deemed as false, it can never be conclusively decided by sequential rationale.

It is completely different when we discuss reality because reality is a condition that must be experienced in order to be authenticated. In other words, judicious abstraction cannot determine if a situation is real because intellectual functions cannot experience. In order to establish if the circumstances described as intrinsic are actual, they must be directly engaged. This is because only the human entity can discern, while faculties necessarily function indirectly.

The exercise of discernment is established upon direct engagement and not upon abstract calculation. Therefore, the perspective of the human entity itself is superior to the corporeal faculty because we possess an inherent overview that deliberation cannot accommodate. Furthermore, rationale evaluates situations piecemeal for the same reason. That is because logic does not have overview things must be reduced to resemble calculable analogies. Consequently, if we need to make a wise and not merely calculated decision, we embrace far more factors and considerations through discernment than we would by following a logical model. Furthermore, by virtue of the determination to make a wise resolution, we necessarily, desire an ethical one because in this sense the two become synonymous.

A sufficiently convincing belief-system that appeals logically and reassures our feeling-sentience, may possess polemical merit but it pales in comparison to the immediate experience of reality. If a religious perspective claims a monopolistic supremacy as to what constitutes reality but describes that condition in solely physical terms, it is inevitably erroneous. Similarly, a philosophical position founded upon erudite, sequential expostulation, however well-established the scholarship, cannot portray reality because reality is neither discovered nor revealed through deduction. Reality is either known through immediate experience, or it remains unrecognized.

The condition of reality that we experience imminently through our authentic identity, must be directly engaged in order to be discovered. Reality is a circumstance, indescribable in physical terms although our experience of it may be conveyed through figurative and metaphoric depiction. Thus, in order to describe the intrinsic existence of a color, we must apply the metaphorical representation of an artistic medium. A numerical depiction does not even remotely approach the reality.

It is regrettable that we have conceded a monopoly of existential interpretation to the authority of materialistically established science and an intellectual theology. We have relinquished our potential, cognitive autonomy to the jurisdiction of scholarship. This is an unbelievably reckless thing to do. Every human being possesses a unique singularity of existence that needs to be experientially discovered, yet we find ourselves misled by the perspectives of those who are ignorant of reality but purport to possess a prerogative concerning it.

A construct, whether theological or philosophical, when juxtaposed to the immediate experience of a condition, is inevitably found wanting. The contrived approach, however logical, simply cannot correspond with direct, experiential knowledge because direct cognition concerns the way things profoundly exist. Consequently, we recognize immediately when we are confronted with an abstract or imaginative interpretation of existence because we are aware of what essential existence is like.

The essential state of the existence of something cannot be portrayed in physical terms because the physical is only a superficial representation. Thus, the complete significance of a phenomenon lies in the intangible dimension whereby it is intrinsically distinguished. Consequently, when we attempt to describe something in terms that refer exclusively to its superficial condition, it appears unconvincing from the point of view of our essential nature. The intellect deals efficiently with physically verifiable evidence but as a function, without the capacity of direct engagement possessed by an entity, it can only manage the superficial properties of things.

If we endeavor to portray the intangible distinction of a phenomenon such as a color, figuratively, it is readily comprehensible to the ipseity of our existence because our authentic identity corresponds in representative language. Inevitably, the representative language of an artistic medium is not limited to the physical appearances of things but describes them in the full dimensionality of their existence.

The intrinsic existence of something is fully recognizable to the human quintessence but an intellectual evaluation, whether in terms of theology or philosophy, is found to be, by comparison, severely wanting. The distinction between the physical representation of a thing and the intrinsic, intangible existence of phenomena, concerns superficiality as opposed to the essential volume wherein the meaningfulness of things reside. Consequently, the complete identity is found when the human quiddity immediately engages the appearance of a thing and discovers the full significance of its existence.

9. THE SIGNIFICANCE OF CONTENT

Absent from usual observation and reflection, and lacking from feeling and subjective evaluation, is the cognitive dimension inherently available to us when we established our singular existence as our perceptive precedence. Conventionally, the authentic identity of the human being is overlooked in favor of corporeal faculties and the observer interprets phenomena in terms of a particular understanding that feels most appropriate. Thereby, we assess circumstances upon the basis of our prior assessment and of our associations and tastes. Consequently, in place of original engagement, we depend upon establish prejudices according to which we endeavor to evaluate all that we encounter. Our conclusions are, for this reason, unoriginal and conventional through the influence of a pre-established mentality. Clearly, we can never discover the authentic condition of things while we anticipate their status beforehand.

Intellectual evaluation and assessment, subjective appraisal and the association of phenomena with familiar, previous circumstances, establishes a dubious substitution for original, cognitive engagement. Conventional cognition of this nature, can never offer unprecedented information but will always, merely, elaborate on extant intelligence.

But our own evaluation of phenomena is of little

interest when we desire to know what the independent existence of something really is. In order to discover the autonomous condition of a phenomenon, we must, necessarily, approach it with scrupulous impartiality. However, the only way that we can engage a condition, uninfluenced by our own pre-conceptual standpoint, is to restrain the human, interpretative faculties and encounter things from the perspective of our own singular significance of existence.

As an incorporeal entity, the essential human being inhabits a condition, not of superficiality but of comprehensive significance. The superficial is easily recognized as the physical semblance, while the essential condition is composed of the entire meaningfulness of a phenomenon. Furthermore, the meaningful is not found in the appearance because value and essential significance are intangible, qualitative realities. They cannot be measured in the manner of a shape or analyzed for their material composition. Yet, it remains difficult for the observer, convinced of the exclusivity of material substance, to recognize the existence of the intangible value of things. However, the intangible significance of a phenomenon reveals its authentic distinction.

The human identity is thought by materialistic, Western philosophy, to be composed merely of its material substance and concomitant functions. This partiality, predictably, restrains cognition within corresponding limits. Thus, we find that our self-constituted antecedence of material exclusivity, together with a determined diminution of the significance of the human being, effectively renders us, existentially meaningless.

The ipseity of the human being is recognized when conventional cognition is postponed. It is discovered to exist, not through reason, but experientially. Thus, the same elemental condition occupied by our essential selves is similarly inhabited by the intangible merit of everything else. That is to say, just as the discovery of the authentic and substantial significance of the human being is hindered through an intrusive materialistic prejudice, so also the phenomenal appearance belies the intrinsic significance of its existence.

In terms of artistic portrayal, the authentic nature of existence is only successfully revealed to the degree that it alludes to the greater significance of an otherwise, merely, superficial appearance. Every artistic work of value suggests the existence of a more profound, intangible dimensionality to the physical and endeavors to present phenomena as they are, not trivially and meaninglessly, but as they exist intrinsically.

The excellence of an artistic endeavor, however, does not merely lie in the superiority of the production, but in the successful articulation of the condition that is experienced through the immediate engagement of the human quintessence. Knowledge of the manner in which things exist in reality, is of greater value and significance than a beautifully executed work. Indeed, it is the experiential recognition of intangible reality that takes our breath away.

It is of little value to attempt to discover the significance of something from the perspective of preconceived notions concerning it. It is through our conventional, intellectual obliqueness that uncertainty concerning the authentic nature of things arises in the first place. Consequently, we imagine that if we amass vast scholarship we demonstrate a superior knowledge of existence than the lesser educated. In reality, much secondhand scholarship is akin to indoctrination because it is not personally discovered and verified but merely, borrowed and emulated. Predictably, the immediate experience of a phenomenon is hindered if we imagine that erudition takes precedence over directly acquired knowledge.

If we wish to discover the intrinsic significance of a thing and it is irrelevant what we preconceive or imagine it to be. Therefore, the artist who attempts to articulate an abstract philosophical construct as if it were reality, offers merely a fiction. That is to say, the juxtaposition between the immediate experience of existence as the content of a work of art, and a hypothetical position that is humanly devised, reveals the significance of the intrinsic condition and the frailty of the speculation.

To the degree that we become familiar with the essential condition of existence, the more easily we differentiate between reality and fiction, and we become aware of the scarceness of such an aptitude. However, lacking familiarity with the authentic condition of things we may imagine that scholarship and expertise offer us an alternative wisdom. But there is no wisdom comparable to that founded upon direct, experiential knowledge. Consequently, our exposure to the crucial condition of existence becomes increasingly established within us as a standard against which all other things may be evaluated.

A subjective interpretation of a condition will, inevitably, distort our view and the real situation will remain obscure. Accordingly, we must set aside feeling-sentience and preference because we wish to discover the actual circumstances of the existence of something.

The singular significance of the human being is the intrinsic distinction. The particular selfhood that intrinsically distinguishes one human being from another, engages everything from a position of its wholly unique individuality. That is to say, the perspective from which the human ipseity experiences things, is its original existence. It is through the unique and individual condition of our existence that we are able to engage phenomena immediately and straightforwardly, and discover the elemental manner of their particular existence.

When we establish a direct experience of the condition of reality as the primary criterion of authenticity, we are able to identify the remoteness of abstract intellectualism, the contrived nature of the philosophical or religious model, and the impoverishment of an exclusively materialistic perspective towards existence.

There is no adequate substitute for immediately ascertained knowledge. The distinction between the actual nature of existence and the fictional alternative, lies between immediate experience and indirect deliberation and deduction. While we apply our imagination in order to speculate upon favorable, conceptual structures founded upon diverse information, and we strive to envisage a tenable outcome, meaningfulness is only properly discovered through direct discernment.

Meanwhile, abstractly conceived conclusions are only based upon the efficiency of our intellect and the value of the available evidence, neither of which are infallible except in terms of mathematics. Consequently, the temptation to try to quantify existence in order to understand it, is enormous.

Nevertheless, the imagination assists invention and explores possible, alternative applications. Even the artist applies imagination in order to discover the optimum manner in which to articulate the content of a composition. But imagination will, inevitably, pollute and distort the substance and content of the work, if it is applied as a means of interpretation. Fictive, extravagant translation will make something seem other than it really is. The masterful application of the language of a particular artistic medium requires considerable discipline and integrity in order to sustain the meaningful content.

The immediate, experiential engagement of phenomena through our essential condition of existence, offers, correspondingly essential knowledge. Immediate cognition, accordingly, must precede communication concerning the profound circumstances of something. In other words, an artistic medium serves us as we strive to articulate intangible significances but if craftsmanship is an end in itself, inevitably, the content will remain insignificant.

Thus, the artist must be quite clear that art is a language through which intangible substance may be revealed because when an artwork is fashioned as an end in itself without articulate content, it remains craft, and however beautifully it may be constructed, it is nevertheless, empty of intrinsic meaning.

Similarly, if the superficial appearance of something is portrayed as the subject of an artwork, it will simply result in a soulless duplicate. Thus, in the same manner whereby the superficial belies the significant, the copyist merely repeats that which is already evident. Consequently, the discovery of the authentic condition of something, as opposed to the superficial appearance, involves the direct experience of the meaning and implication of the object, and not merely the deceptive facade.

    Knowledge concerning intrinsic existence is not achievable through conventional cognition and the artist who is unaware of the intangible substance of a phenomenon, cannot hope to offer a meaningful communication. The exclusive manner whereby the greater significance of the blatant appearance is discovered, is through the direct, perceptual engagement of our singular identity.

    Scarcely anything can be more consequential in terms of all that we do than the recognition of our own individual significance and the establishment of our intrinsic identity as our cognitive perspective towards other people and all phenomena. Thereby, we discover, the multidimensional volume of existence and recognized the intrinsic value inherent to all phenomena.

10. IMMEDIACY

The difficulty concerning intangible evidence is that it is inevitably, only experientially recognizable. Consequently, the existence of the physically elusive conditions concerning the intrinsic significance of a phenomenon cannot be determined in the same manner whereby we ascertain physical situations. Similarly, understanding intangible existence seems essentially disproportionate in contrast to the systematic listing and cataloging of the physical occurrence whose material certainty is without doubt.

Although, through a skillfully executed artistic medium, the nature of intangible existence may be successfully portrayed, the results may not necessarily pertain to reality. Art is a language readily used in the service of fiction as towards the representation of authentic, fundamental circumstances. The use of metaphor and figure may describe an imaginative creation just as effectively as they may be applied to reveal the existence of the intangible significances that are real.

Consensus, similarly, offers little conclusive validation as it is well known how readily persuaded a gathering may be, through enthusiasm and infective concurrence. Thus, a convincing polemic may awaken the eagerness of a congregation and persuade the majority to embrace even the absurd as if it were authentic.

As it stands, the manner whereby the existence of the intangible dimension of physical appearances is verified, lies beyond the reach of conventional cognition. However, it is well within the capability of the human ipseity to engage the physically impalpable because our essential existence does not reside within the material appearance. That is to say, the human essence inhabits the same condition of relevancy as the meaningful and intrinsic impressiveness of all phenomena.

The implications that arise upon the discovery of our human, intangible significance, are enormously profound and far-reaching. Thereby, the experiential recognition of a dimension to phenomena that belies the material appearance, completely reverses our conventional stance towards life. Obviously, we know that we possess a material form, and we have inadvertently identified our existence with our corporeal condition. But our identity is not discovered upon an examination of the physical appearance or its properties and its functions, but it is found to exist independently in its own right.

Further, we find that the practice whereby we conventionally evidence the condition of phenomena, inevitably, maintains an extremely limited perspective towards existence. Not only does the intellect exclusively, indirectly function, and the feeling nature, subjectively, but both approaches are influenced by prejudice. We never really evaluate a phenomenon objectively but consistently appraise it obliquely and select the interpretation that appears the most convincing and the one which we most readily favor. Nevertheless, we cannot avoid the biased approach because the human intellect and feeling-sentience and incapable of definitive resolution.

In order to achieve definitive knowledge concerning intangible circumstances, it is essential to directly experience a situation. And in order to describe profound conditions they must be portrayed metaphorically because that is the language required to describe intrinsic situations. But that is not possible directly engage things through the intellect because, as a calculative function, reason cannot experience.

An encounter must be directly established, and the phenomenon originally engaged through the perspective of our essential person if we wish to ascertain the essential significance. The direct, experiential approach of the human entity avoids the oblique manner of evaluation that has become our conventional, cognitional practice, and which is ideally suited to a stance that predominantly deals with the tangible evidence of things.

Similarly, feeling-sentience is incapable of presenting conclusive evidence because it is, necessarily, subjective, otherwise it would be of little value to us. But subjective, instinctively derived evidence influenced by individual penchant, is neither convincing nor incontrovertible. Consequently, what is required is the establishment of a cognitive approach that engages a situation without distorting the evidence. However, if we deny the existence of our extant, individual continuance and its intrinsic status, then the extent of our knowledge will always remain confined to the material dimension of existence.

In terms of cognition, equally valueless is the selection of a belief or preference that asserts the existence of the intangible value of the human being but otherwise possesses no other basis of certainty.

Indeed, we are not trying to establish another belief-system but we wish to present a cognitive approach whereby we may encounter the authentic condition of things. Beliefs we have aplenty, some more obscure and obviously fictional than others.

In order for the human being to attain cognitional autonomy, whereby the singular nature of our actuality may directly encounter a situation for itself, and through which phenomena and events are discovered in the elemental condition of their existence, the individual, human ipseity must assume its rightful authority. Therefore, the established prerogative assumed by the intellect and feeling-sentience must be withdrawn and reestablished upon the sovereign condition of our individual significance which is the authentic identity of the human being.

The discovery of the human, incorporeally extant identity, is beyond the capacity of deduction to determine. It may be implied, but it will not be found through rational justification based either upon implicit evidence or unverifiable supposition. In other words, through the extremity of conventional, cognitive limitation and the flexible manner of deduction, the existence of the intangible significance of the human being remains beyond the conclusive justification of ordinary recognition. Yet, the incorporeal nature of our existence is the basis upon which immediate cognition as a perceptive approach, is dependent.

The human being recognizes the significance of its own existence that is the singular distinction, through the restraint of our conventional, cognitive faculties. Thereby, each human being discovers the individual nature of their own being. Subsequently, upon immediate engagement, the human essence further pursues the implications of immediate cognition by extending the compass of the research. That is to say, our inquiries extend from immediate self-recognition to the positioning of the ipseity as the optimum point of view. Consequently, from the perspective of our own singularity, the essential condition of all other things becomes, correspondingly, self-evident.

It is entirely possible for someone to remain ignorant of their authentic identity and assume that their corporeal condition is the extent of their existence. Consequently, they will never discover the existential significance of phenomena, and they will remain cognitively circumscribed within physical superficiality.

Undoubtedly, the staunch materialist is not convinced through persuasion of the authenticity of an elusive intrinsicality, even though the intangible, qualitative dimension of physical appearances is blatantly manifest through experience. But experiential evidence is not readily justified nor quantified for the convenience of the intellect and, consequently, while recognized, intangible value cannot be conclusively justified as extant.

We experience the essential qualities of phenomena all the time but because of their intangible nature, materialistic, Western philosophy discounts them entirely from its interpretation of existence. The result is a meaningless construct without dimension or value.

To be fair, the materialist does not entirely deny the existence of the qualitative dimension of phenomena but philosophically separates it from the physical appearance, as if the physical existed in isolation. Consequently, the incorporeal value of something continues to be experientially acknowledged, but an exclusively physical ideology must dismiss it as evidence because it cannot be definitively proven to exist as it is without material pertinence. Therefore, intellectually, the intangible is marginalized while, experientially, it is found to be of vital significance. Accordingly, it remains a conveniently overlooked contradiction.

The materialistic perspective would matter little if we maintained a strong respect for the intangible pertinence of phenomena, but materialistic, Western philosophy has established a ubiquitous and entrenched version of existence that is not easily dislodged. It does much damage because it maintains an unreal perspective towards existence that is void of significance and value. Materialistic myopia in all its forms and applications is the primary antagonist against human advancement.

Not to be outdone, feeling-sentient subjective knowledge in a credulous and superstitious mind is equally culpable and deceptive. However, an anomalistic conviction does not necessarily pertain to madness but, conceivably, when immediate cognition is attempted without fully understanding that rationale and feeling-sentience must not be allowed to intrude.

However, these things need not be mysterious. We have clearly stated that physical properties alone do not possess existential significance but they exist peripherally to a further intrinsic significance. But while the authenticity of intangible value is readily conceded even by the staunch materialist, the conceit of scholarship and the prestige of erudition prevents open-minded exploration. The convinced materialist, inevitably, finds no evidence to support the qualitative merit of existence because value and meaning exist intangibly. There is no physical evidence to be found, but that is scarcely a basis for the denial of that which experientially recognized as valid. Clearly, the fault lies with materialistic exclusivity as an abstractly contrived approach to comprehensive understanding.

The way forward rests not upon the blind acceptance of the significance of the qualitative dimension of existence but upon a candid examination of intangible merit. Upon empirical research, the conviction will develop that is it not only possible that there exists an intangible depth to phenomena but that it is of a more profound significance than the isolated, superficial appearance. Indeed, a qualitative magnitude exists against which the solitary, physical semblance appears negligible because of its lack of value and meaningfulness. Indeed, the profundity of a phenomenon lies in its intangible significance.

From the recognition of the merit of the intangible significance of things, the existence of the human being may be explored. It is discovered that our own individual value rests not solely with the physical appearance but in that which qualifies our material condition and gives it individual significance. That is to say, that which lends value to an otherwise meaningless and superficial facade, exists intangibly and it remains the origin of the singular identity that essentially distinguishes the existence of one person from another. In other words, that which qualifies the generic human body as the particular, essential individual that is you, or I, exists intangibly but it can be discerned through immediate cognition.

It is soon evident to the openminded researcher that the significance of the human being and that which determines the individual status of our existence, is not physically dependent but exists incorporeally. This becomes known when we recognize that the body itself is not an entity but it possesses significance only when it is qualified through the intangible singularity of the human being. Thereby, the human essence is acknowledged through immediate, experiential cognition as the intrinsic significance of our constitution and thereafter established as the seat of our cognitive determination.

11. THE QUALITATIVE DISTINCTION

From the artist's point of view, if one wishes to capture the essential distinction of a subject, a scrutiny of the infinite detail of the appearance will hinder a grasp of the significance. This is because the condition of the existence of something is not exclusively physical but both essential and biographic.

A color possesses only marginal physicality and, consequently, the material sciences have difficulty adequately representing it and imagine that a numerical value or rarefied equivalency somehow depicts the entirety. The attempted quantification of something such as light, that exists essentially with only implied representation, necessarily overlooks the authentic condition of the existence of the phenomenon.

It is remarkable how common the abstract manner of phenomenal evaluation is. A situation is not necessarily viewed objectively as expected, but through the lens of an abstractly contrived philosophy that subsequently constrains and deforms it.

For example, the immediate experience of a color reveals that its connotation is physically illusive, nevertheless, the conviction that everything significant must be reduced and explained in physical terms persists because, abstractly, we are convinced that the entire substance of a phenomenon is physical. This has become an established mindset which overrides direct, experiential knowledge and many knowledgeable people find themselves entirely satisfied with an equation or a formula that purports to explain, for example, the color red, in terms of energy.

Similarly, in terms of organic life, it is imagined that creatures can be explained through their mechanical, chemical and electrical properties merely because physical activities are readily identifiable and may be decisively calibrated.

The origin of an organism is thought to be material and tremendous imaginative effort is applied in the attempt to conceive and coherently explain how organization could have spontaneously occurred. Conveniently, abstract rationale, remote from an immediate experience of the phenomenal event, is free to imaginatively manipulate, selectively applicable information into a contrived construct. If the conclusion is pertinent to the evidence, appears reasonable and is well argued, it earns the approval and consensus of the learned community.

Nevertheless, the oblique estimation of probabilities, founded upon the exclusive evidence of physical properties, is no match for immediate experience because the abstract condition in which reason operates remains remote from the actual event. Therefore, the state of the existence of something is discovered neither through an analysis of physical minutiae nor by abstract conceptualization.

However, the fine artist discovers and portrays the essential identity of something through an immediate, cognitional engagement of the entirety of the existence of the phenomenon. That is to say, significance is found to reside in the entirety of something which includes its elemental condition and its inherent identity. Using the former example, the color red possesses a unique qualitative existence that is unrecognizable in terms of mathematical representation.

Similarly, the significance of a particular organism lies in its intrinsic nature and not exclusively in the subsequential, physical appearance. The essential existence of a creature is discovered to exist intangibly as a compound, qualitative expression, while the appearance is governed directly through ambient law and by an animal's subjective response to immediate ecological influences. Thus, we recognize two classes of phenomena. That is, the color red possesses inherent permanency that remains its distinction regardless of the context or circumstances, while the organism possesses conceptual generality and interpretative flexibility.

Organic, conceptual generality is, necessarily, intentional both in terms of the humanly manufactured item and in Nature. Conversely, random, capricious amalgamation without an objective, is meaningless and insignificant because disordered influences are inevitably chaotic. Nevertheless, the abstract philosopher is determined that commonsense be abandoned in favor of a contrived explanation of life.

Regularity and order of the magnitude of a life-form imply a progressive symmetry of activities towards a very specific outcome. Indeed, should the functions of an organism suddenly behave erratically and unpredictably, chaos immediately ensues and the creature disintegrates. Thus, if order is withdrawn, the living thing ceases to be viable. Its constitution is compromised and, consequently, it is no longer a tenable life-form. Thus, the recognition of imperative order is indicative of general, conceptual arrangement.

No one will seriously deny the existence of organic order and arrangement because we all know what happens when structure and paradigmatic conformation are abandoned. However, the materialist takes exception to the suggestion that organic organization is intentional because material evidence does not appear to indicate a conceptual inception.

In terms of human invention, it is readily evident that a human mind conceives a certain plan and constitutional arrangement in order to fabricate a product. And without a plan, there is chaos. But in Nature, no such origin is apparent. Thus, the materialist is mystified. Obviously order exists but it is without evident origination and, consequently, the attempt is made to explore the possibility of spontaneous, organic organization whereby, through the influence of ambient ecological forces, the meticulous coalescence of materials and physics, produces, working and reproducing organic symmetry.

This scenario is satisfactory only to an abstractly preoccupied mentality, and it is immediately dispersed when we consider the complexity of organic organization and the fragility of its maintenance. An organism cannot sustain life if it is compromised and, consequently, it must have always been in a condition of tenability or otherwise, nonexistence. There is no such thing as a partially functioning organism. It is either complete or it is without cohesion.

It is the consistently functional coherence of organic organization, in all its diversity, that reveals the existence of conceptual origin and its continued maintenance. There are no errors nor oversights. The essential performances and inter-workings of organisms are immaculate and remain so as the creature moves through a diversity of appearances.

Similarly, the manner whereby an animal or plant metamorphically assumes a particular physiognomy towards a very distinct end and subsequently appears quite different in order to fulfill an alternative function, is evidence of intention. That is to say, an extraordinarily complex conceptual structure exists as the impetus of a metamorphic transformation.

Therefore, an entire creature may be refashioned from a terrestrial condition to the aerial as in the case of the butterfly, or in terms of mammalian embryology, the same biomaterial is constantly, metamorphically transformed in order to achieve its conceptual maturity, only to be concentrated once more into the minuscule condition and intensity of the egg. Thereupon, common biomaterial is again, metamorphically transformed in the service of the entire conceptual structure of a plant and appears as root, stem, leaf or seed. Indeed, the dynamic of growth-transformation is always metamorphic. That is to say is no such thing as growth as mere enlargement but only metamorphic progression.

If an organism is imagined as defined merely through a scrutiny of its infinitesimal material detail and physical workings, the conceptual origin will be overlooked. The intrinsic nature of the existence of something is not found in the way it appears to function but only when the completeness of a phenomenon is discovered for what it is. In other words, the measurement of isolated physical properties and the examination of processes cannot reveal the identity of the entirety because how something works does not unmask its particular distinction.

The human being discovers the conceptual origin and intentional dynamics of organic life to the degree that natural events are immediately and open-mindedly explored without the encumbrance of materialistic prejudice. Materialistic exclusivity is a misleading philosophy because it presumes that existence is entirely physical and, consequently, it overlooks intangible significances such as conceptual origin and intention, that reveal the authentic condition of phenomena.

For example, the explicit distinction of a carrot compared, for example, to that of a potato, is not adequately represented by the differences of their chemical composition, nor through an examination of their cellular mechanics. The significance of the carrot, as opposed to the potato, lies in the manner whereby the common vegetable nature that they share, is particularly realized. Both vegetables possess the same plant concept, firstly expressed as a root crop and specifically pronounced as carrot and potato.

The carrot differentiation is obviously recognizable through its physical appearance, but its intrinsic distinction resides more fundamentally as a particular, qualitative interpretation of the shared vegetable concept. That is to say, the distinction between the carrot and the potato lies in the inherent and characteristic manner whereby the commonalities that define them both as root vegetables, are individually expressed.

To distinguish between the two vegetables merely on the basis of carotene or starch isolates the chemical properties from the entirety. The entire carrot, through every facet, detail and fiber of its embodiment, expresses the particular qualitative declaration that differentiates it from the potato. In this sense, the qualitative merit of a phenomenon remains elusive to physical analysis and scrutiny because while the material appearance reproduces the manner whereby one organism differentiates from another, it does not specifically manifest the entirety of that distinction. The distinction that identifies a carrot from a potato is intangible alike to all qualities and values. But it is the physically elusive, qualitative distinction that determines the particular manner of the physical appearance.

In terms of immediate observation, if one views nature through the eye of the colorist, one discovers the subtleties of the colored world. Similarly, if we observe the stresses, tensions and gestures of physical form, we recognize the sculptural dynamics of objects. Meanwhile, the poet searches out the character, disposition and complexion of phenomena and describes subtle qualitative values through a particular artistic medium.

Engaging phenomena directly and plainly, in search of their substantive value, whether that be the essential value of a color, the sculptural motion and form gesture and the particular stance and expression of a creature, or the inherent temper whereby something attests to its intrinsic identity; the distinction of a phenomenon is correctly recognized through the quality of its manner of expression.

That is to say, the qualitative condition of the existence of an organism, is its authentic identity. The physical appearance alone does not reveal the overarching particularity that distinguishes between phenomena because the qualitative significance is the origin and not the subsequence of the physical occurrence. If it were otherwise, it would be as if a painting or photograph were the reality while the content or subject was summarily dismissed as of marginal consequence.

12. IMMEDIATE ENGAGEMENT

If we fail to experientially recognize our own uniqueness of existence, we cannot determine the inherent individuality of another person nor apprehend the nature of the essential existence of phenomena. This is because, the unique distinction of existence possessed by every human being, resides in an original, essential condition. There is nothing that separates the human singularity of existence from the intrinsic nature of phenomena because both the human essence and the intrinsic condition of other things, exist in the same incorporeal circumstances.

Without the direct engagement of our singular originality of being, we evaluate phenomena indirectly through our lesser cognitive faculties of feeling-sentience and by oblique, intellectual assessment. Feeling-sentience is always subjective, while reason functions only after the event or abstractly, imaginatively devising possible explanations. We are unable to engage circumstances straightforwardly through these circuitous practices and, consequently, fail to discover phenomena in their elemental condition.

Our singular originality of being exists essentially in its own right, independent of corporeal circumstances. It resides in a state of immediacy towards all other phenomena. The direct approach is only possible through the unique singularity and constant, existential condition of the human being. Our essential identity is able to approach phenomena immediately and decisively. Nothing separates the human, singularity of existence from the essential substance of a phenomenon and, consequently, the authentic condition of something is instantaneously evident.

Everything is found as it exists elementally when the human quintessence engages phenomena instantly without the interpretative interference of the corporeal faculties of cognition. Nothing is permitted to substitute for immediate cognition. Feeling-sentience, however heightened our instincts may be developed, merely detracts; while the sharpest and most astute, intellectual proficiency remains inexplicit in the face of immediate knowledge.

Only the authentic, human identity is able to engage circumstances directly. Corporeal faculties are not entities but capabilities and instruments associated with the body. An entity may experience but a faculty cannot. It is through imminent experience that the human singularity of existence discovers the essential condition of phenomena. Recognition of the authentic manner of the existence of things becomes increasingly compelling because we discover what things are intrinsically, which is the authentic condition of their existence. Further, we find that our correspondence with them becomes appropriate.

The imminent engagement of phenomena

through the straightforward, experiential approach of the human, quiddity, establishes a condition whereby things are discovered in the manner wherein they exist elementally. Elemental implies a state of existential originality before our human faculties of rational deduction and feeling-sentience are able to distort our perception through their interpretive processes. Thus, the intellect must be restrained and the feeling nature of the human being must be quieted and permitted to be influenced by the profundity of existence, whereby it is elevated from vacillation and waver, towards confidence.

There is nothing mysterious or supernatural about the renewal of the human soul in this manner. It is the inevitable consequence of the immediate experience of reality that influences our feeling condition and imbues it with balance. We discover through direct cognition that our existence is substantially founded and not merely corporeal and transient. Consequently, our feeling condition becomes reassured not through intellectual persuasion nor through attempted, emotional self-restoration, but because we encounter the condition wherein everything is authentic.

Through every corporeal sense, the human essence discovers the existential status of all phenomena but we do not rely on sense-information as a scientist would an instrument or a monitor. The human being, in its quintessential condition engages sense-information not circuitously, as if through wires and measuring devices, but immediately. The human essence encounters all circumstances directly and through its essential condition it discovers only authenticity because it penetrates to the elemental and original condition of things. Consequently, the exactitude of physically derived data is irrelevant because it is not the appearance that interest the human essence, but the absolute. The physical appearance merely serves as a focus of attention but the human quintessence delves immediately into the substance of phenomena and discovers the full dimensionality of their existence.

    The crux of the essential approach lies in the immediate manner whereby phenomena are engaged. This is only possible, through direct cognition by the human, quintessential singularity of existence. The raw identity of the human being encounters phenomena as they are in reality and not as we suppose, imagine or prefer them to be. Thus, the feeling nature is restored through the experience of reality and its tendency to indulge itself is ameliorated by exposure to the substantial condition of existence. Meanwhile, theological conviction and abstract, deductive rationale are restrained in order that the encounter between the human quintessence and phenomena remains direct and unalloyed through preconceptual bias.

13. EXPERIENTIAL ENCOUNTER

The only way to discover the condition of reality is through experiential encounter. Reality is intellectually elusive because conceptualization is inevitably an indirect practice. We cannot know something through rationale that is solely accessible through experience. We may speculate concerning the nature of a condition but unless we are immediately exposed to it, we cannot assume to have apprehended it with adequate justification.

Similarly, the direct approach is misunderstood if it is assumed that it is merely an attentive and heightened activity of the senses. The dynamic of immediate cognition is incorporeally effective and requires that the quintessential identity of the human being, that exists without physical representation, directly encounter the material condition of a phenomenon and discover its intangible significance.

The manner whereby we typically negotiate the events and circumstances of life, rests upon our favored and practiced cognitive approach. Influenced by conviction, whether it be empirically derived or founded upon revelation, we inevitably avoid the immediate experience of phenomena. We imagine that we know something concerning reality upon the basis of our extensive scholarship and education, a position that assumes that knowledge of the condition of authenticity is only available to those of conspicuous learning. Thus, we find individuals who effusively demonstrate the scope of their abstract knowledge thereby reveal their ignorance of the extant circumstances because they are without immediate experience.

Whatever the dominant conceptual structure may be, inevitably, it will be accompanied by myriad other pre-established convictions that obscure our discovery of the authentic condition of phenomena. Content with what we imagine and feel that we know, we neglect to elicit definitive knowledge concerning something from the actual condition itself. Thus, we hinder our own inquiry through presupposition and preoccupation with established concepts and abstract conceptualization.

The incorporeal and significant identity of the human being it able to engage and discover the intrinsic nature of the existence of phenomena, through immediate cognition. The human quiddity avoids the self-deception created through presupposition because it exists essentially and independently of the corporeal faculties. It does not rely upon abstractly conceived interpretations concerning the nature of phenomena nor it is persuaded by the doctrinal perspectives of theology and specialized scholarship.

Lest the atheistic stance should imagine itself invulnerable and aloof through its indifferent approach towards incorporeal existence, atheism remains a doctrinal prejudice like any other. It is one that is frequently defended with greater fervor than the position of those possessed of a moderate and inoffensive devotion towards Deity.

Any pre-conceptual stance towards existence obstructs a direct, cognitive approach between the human quiddity and the phenomenon. Presupposed convictions always ensure that a situation will be viewed from the perspective of a particular philosophical prejudice and, inevitably, original experience will be obscured. A preferred position may be championed and shielded as thoroughly defensible by peer consensus, yet remain inconclusive in its argument and consequently reveal an ultimate reliance on conviction rather than evidence. Logic, unlike mathematics, is flexible. It purports to follow dialectic to its reasonable conclusion but it does not possess the capacity of definitive exactitude. Its seems to proceed with apparent precision but rationalism can never approach the conclusiveness of the calculation. Ultimately, it will always remain selective in its resolution.

The supposed numerical equivalency of a phenomenon, through its attempted reduction into calculable terms, is always, only partly achievable. Inevitably, the bulk of the phenomenal evidence remains marginalized because quantification is only a measure and not a distillation. We deceive ourselves if we imagine that a quantity can sufficiently represent the entirety of a phenomenon. The approach that relies on quantification as the definitive justification of an otherwise elusive value merely assumes an authoritative position over feeling-sentient subjectivity. In reality, quantification is similarly inadequate if it supposes that computable properties define the full extent of something. The measurement of anything will always be only a mathematically abstract representation of those exclusive aspects of a phenomenon that can be measured. Measurements do not exist independently of the phenomenon and they do not reveal what something actually is. The potential deception that imagines that a thing is represented by the manner of its measurement, appears to be avoidable if we assume that the researcher appends the caveat that their equations represent merely an abstract aspect of a phenomenon. But in practice, the mathematical model is allowed to take precedence and assumes a deceptive reality of its own.

When something is immediately engaged and our inherent and adopted predilections are restrained, we discover the extant condition. We encounter phenomena directly upon their own terms. However, the immediate engagement must be conducted from the perspective of the human quiddity because the absolute condition of the existence of something is only discovered from the unsullied and original perspective of the incorporeal distinction of the human being.

The condition in which the human, incorporeal quiddity exists is reality. It is through the experiential knowledge of the nature of reality that all other things may be assessed for their ultimate authenticity. The human quiddity is the sovereign identity of the human being and the benchmark of legitimacy against which all doctrine, conjecture and conviction may be evaluated for its significance.

14. INTELLECTUAL MINIMIZATION

An assumed, autocratic monopoly concerning the nature of existence has become adopted by the technical specialist. Unchallenged because the layman is hopelessly ill-equipped to counter the assertions of the technician, the expert presumes the position of final arbiter in matters both great and small. Thus, a technical, philosophical view of existence has become grafted upon human understanding that is frequently at odds even with common sense.

The opinion of the expert in almost any field, is readily granted an elevated status and the decrees of the learned minority influence the outlook of the apparently ignorant majority. Even in matters beyond the extent of a particular specialty, it is assumed that because their intellects function in an ostensibly systematic manner, they possess a superior prerogative. That their position and stance merely represents opinion and not expertise fails to raise concern and the technical specialist is permitted free rein to publicly pronounce on all matters with authority.

Thus, we find technical experts intruding into areas in which they have neither experience nor knowledge, because they are assumed to possess elevated insight in all matters existential. They preoccupy themselves with the technicality of their particular forte and imagine that they are thereby qualified to adjudicate concerning the macrocosm and that they comprehend the entirety of existence.

Formerly, in centuries past, this position was occupied by the priesthood who were the authorities of revelation in all things spiritual. It was imagined that with the advent of objective reason that the human being would become emancipated from the despotic subjugation of presupposed authority. But this progressive potential has been thwarted through a peculiar materialistic reversal that has instead bequeathed jurisdiction to the scientific establishment and once more usurped individual prerogative.

Fortunately, there resides as the essential constitution of the human being, the capacity to experience and know reality for oneself. The independent development of a knowledge of that which is ultimately authentic is the immanent gateway to human, cognitional autonomy. The authenticity of the intangible uniqueness of the human individual, while denied by materialistic, Western philosophy, is nonetheless experientially justifiable to everyone because it is the intrinsic condition of our existence.

Every person and phenomenon is an individual statement of the manner of their existence. It is the individual condition that we discover through direct cognitive engagement by our own authentic identity.

It is extraordinary that we do not continually wonder about the human condition and our Earthly context because it merits considerable astonishment. The original approach without presupposition, fosters surprise and provokes a fresh perspective whereby all things are experienced with the fascination of one who wishes to learn, not monochromatically as the abstract reductionist considers existence but comprehensively.

Further, wonder is not merely the pleasure occasioned by the majesty of a beautiful landscape or the awe we feel at the myriad, strikingly colorful and distinctive creatures and plants that populate the earth, but it is born of a cognitive rearrangement whereby all things are experienced uniquely and originally, as if for the very first time. The human quiddity of existence engages everything in this manner and it is the actuality of phenomenal existence that instills a profound amazement because we recognize that these things do not merely exist in terms of our off-hand, abstract interpretation of them but in actually. They strike us as enormously wonderful not because they are beautiful or intriguing but because they are real.

It is far better to retain astonishment than to endeavor to rationalize a perplexing situation through conjecture. The attempt to address the extraordinariness of the reality of our human and phenomenal existence in terms that minimize their significance, trivializes something that is better merely encountered with alertness than explained away.

When we approach existence without endeavoring

to decipher things intellectually or evaluate them subjectively, we meet the circumstances of our human condition, straightforwardly. The human being, when the corporeal faculties are restrained, is able to confront every situation of our existence uniquely without preconceptual and evaluative interference. Through unique engagement it becomes evident that the very appropriate stance of wonder promotes original cognition. Unhampered by imaginative, abstract supposition that cleverly negates the existential significance of perplexing phenomena and otherwise unusual circumstances and, untrammeled by feeling-sentient evaluation, the experience remains original between the human quiddity and the phenomenon. Thus, we face a mysterious and surprising condition straightforwardly and discover the nature of existence through a profound and immediate event of cognition.

When phenomena are engaged in this direct manner, a distinction becomes evident between the superficial appearance of something and its authentic substance. The appearance is acknowledged as merely transient while the substance is found to exist intangibly. Every phenomenon is recognized for the condition of its intrinsic existence.

If, for example, we engage organic phenomena originally from the perspective of our quiddity, that is the individual uniqueness of our existence, we establish significant knowledge through the sense of wonder that arises from our direct engagement of things and our experiential recognition of their authenticity. We find that the origin of an organic structure does not reside within its physical condition but that it exists conceptually. The materials of its establishment serve the dictates of the concept but of themselves, they do not posses creative ability.

Similarly, Natural forces that we identify and which bear upon and define the general parameters of the appearances of creatures, are not conceptually active but they are the blind coordinates of the earthly context. They are without inventive competency. Only an entity possesses creativity and, consequently, the conceptual origin of organic phenomena will not be found amongst elemental forces nor their particular, regulatory influences.

Through the unique encounter between the human, essential individuality and the organic phenomenon, we recognize the activity of conceptualization because we posses the same capacity ourselves. Similarly, we know when it is not apparent and where creativity does not exist. Yet, the intellectual materialist will stubbornly insist that organic organization arises through capricious, sightless forces and organization and genius reside within the innate.

This refusal to restrain the habitual practice of the intellectual minimization of existence, is predictable considering the invested scholarship of the clerisy. The only recourse for the individual is to withdraw the monopolistic status that has been afforded to the intelligentsia and leave them to their own devices while we explore and move forward towards a greater grasp of the substantial and the meaningful significances of existence.

15. THE THIRD COGNITIVE APPROACH

The skeptic, steeped in the traditions of abstract intellectual doctrine, imagines that there exists merely two calibers of human cognition because no serious value is attributed by materialistic Western philosophy to intangible significances. The human quiddity exists incorporeally and, consequently, its reality is emphatically denied. Both of the conventional cognitive practices rely upon accumulated, prior evidence concerning phenomena and neither is able to engage a situation originally. Either something is subjectively evaluated through our feeling-sentient nature or its material condition is analyzed and reduced into terms resembling the mathematical equation whereby the intellect may confidently evaluate and determine its significance.

As we have already explored, intangible value can never be entirely represented through the physical appearance and, consequently, reduction and subsequent quantification fails to reveal qualitative significances and nuances that essentially distinguish one phenomenon from another. Qualities and values are, consequently, misdefined and their significance lost because it is erroneously assumed that their importance can be entirely quantified or that they exist merely as a qualification of the physical.

If it were true that the material appearance alone possessed consequence and that the qualitative value of a phenomenon was negligible, then the resulting manifestation would not resemble our experience. It would be devoid of essential meaning and intangible significance.

The qualitative value of something is indicative of the intrinsic condition of its existence yet, it remains physically unrepresented. If it is assumed that the intangible, qualitative condition is unimportant and irrelevant to the existence of a phenomenon then the inherent value and intrinsic identity of a thing will be entirely overlooked. We are merely left with the superficial appearance that is without consequence.

Conversely, if the materialist concedes value and substance to the intangible, qualitative dimension of a phenomenon then materialistic exclusivity as a philosophical approach, is shattered because all intangible significances must be similarly included and considered. Therefore, the incorporeal human quiddity would be accepted as possessing a comparable significance and existence as the intangible qualitative value of something because they are of a similar denomination. Thus, it is recognized that either materialism must deny intangible value entirely or acknowledge that materialistic Western philosophy is merely an untenable and contrived belief, remote from reality.

A third cognitive method exists that is quite distinct from the intellectual and the feeling-sentient approaches. It is the only cognitive practice to reveal conclusive evidence concerning the intangible, intrinsic significance of things. The two conventional practices cannot successfully identify and qualify the intangible. Feeling-sentience is always subjective while the popular preponderance of the intellectual approach in matters of evaluation must, necessarily, deny the authenticity of an intangible existence because incorporeal reality cannot be favorably demonstrated as extant through reason alone.

Intangible significances, however, are readily identified through experience but in order that they may be justified it is essential that the human quiddity be established as the entity doing the experiencing. This is vital because otherwise experience remains merely subjective. The human quiddity, however, is not the feeling nature but the authentic identity. The human entity alone is capable of direct engagement and discovers thereby the absolute authenticity of itself. It is from the perspective of the absolute authenticity of the human entity that the intangible substance of phenomena are discovered. The human quiddity knows reality because it is itself, ultimately real. That is to say, the authentic and intangible condition of existence of the human being is alone capable of definitive judgment because it is ultimately authentic and exists not as a corporeal faculty but as an entity.

While the testimony of the human feeling-sentient

nature is easily challenged through its prevalent subjectivity, the human quiddity experientially knows the authentic condition of reality because it exists elementally and originally and, consequently, it inhabits a condition of permanence. The transient nature of material appearances connotes a superficiality that the human quiddity could never accept as the authentic condition of a phenomenon. Consequently, the immutable human essence is able to pierce through the appearance and recognize the substantial condition of a phenomenon which it discovers to be intangible like itself.

This position is dismissed by conventional scholarship. Most philosophical positions are not experientially and personally founded through one's own research, but they are adopted. Almost every perspective and conviction is established upon someone else's opinion. A position is studied and if it is found to be agreeable then it is taken as one's own. It is imagined that a point-of-view is more significantly validated if it is found to be the corroborated opinion and conclusion of others. There is seldom any original work but merely the appropriation of the works and convictions of someone else.

For example, we have the absurd situation wherein one faction supports a Creationist philosophical model while another supports a neo-Darwinist approach. A third party endeavors to span the two contrary positions through an amalgamation and insists that Creative

Intelligence is the most satisfactory explanation of human and phenomenal existence.

It is indicative of the shallowness of the debate and the disingenuous pretension of choosing a point of view instead of remaining open-minded, that there appears to exist merely three possible selections. If the matter were to be approached originally and experientially though the aegis of the human quiddity, the irrelevance of all three would be self-evident because they would all be recognized as abstractly conceived. They would be seen as speculative and not experientially and directly related to the condition of reality at all.

We steadfastly maintain positions that are not of our own formulation and, consequently, we fail to explore an original perspective but instead, merely follow the lead of another. Very few who maintain a philosophical position towards existence, have arrived there of their own volition. They have not explored life for themselves but merely adopt expertise and opinions that are of extraneous origin. If an approach is sufficiently of convincing merit and appeals to their particular mentality and bias, then it is embraced, championed and defended.

There is no autonomy whatsoever in selecting an already established perspective. It is the burden of every individual to arrive at an original, self-determined position towards existence, otherwise we inevitably remain in a condition of cognitive bondage and self-determination is forever elusive.

122

16. THE AUTHENTIC, HUMAN CONDITION

An original and un-jaded perspective, uninfluenced by conceptual presupposition, permits the human, actuality of existence to directly experience its own substantiality and, subsequently, discover the intangible significance that is overlooked when the physical appearance is assumed to be the extent of a phenomenon.

A structure or construct is inevitably contrived and even though it may be exquisitely reasoned. It will always pale beside the results of immediate cognition because the human being as an entity, is able to experientially engage phenomena while the faculty of reason, as a function, works obliquely. An adopted authority of any nature, whether it be a conceptual structure that endeavors to explain existence or a belief system that is founded upon revelation, inevitably detracts from the development of individual, sovereign autonomy. The individual must become experientially familiar with the astonishing reality and significance of the singular existence of the human being. The implications of the direct discovery of the human essence include knowledge concerning the incorporeal and intransient condition of the essential human being which is further compounded by the recognition of the similarly unique status of all other people.

But the greater consequence rests upon the

discovery that, through our constant, existential condition that exists in a situation of immediacy, we are able to determine the inherent significance of all other phenomena. This is knowledge of the highest caliber because it is experientially discovered through the human entity itself and not merely by virtue of intellectual faculties or feeling-sentience. No one can achieve immediate cognition on our behalf because it directly involves our authentic identity as the cognitive perspective from which the legitimate state of the existence of things is conclusively discovered.

A humanly fabricated explanation of existence will inevitably remain abstract in the sense that it is conceived by our human faculties and not directly recognized by the human entity itself. Furthermore, as the abstract structure becomes conviction, it detracts from our progressive development towards autonomy because it superimposes a view of existence that needs to be discovered and known directly and particularly, through immediate engagement.

Any presupposition that assumes that we already possess a conclusive understanding of existence is a hindrance to the discovery of the authentic condition of things. Our apparent familiarity does not rest upon the way things actually are but upon the superficial perspective of our own assumptions and biases.

Immediate cognition is not another path, belief or practice but it is a statement concerning the manner whereby things may be discovered originally, in their elemental condition of existence and not as we think or imagine them to be.

If a person is convinced that feeling-sentience and reason are of themselves sufficient, then definitive knowledge concerning existence will remain unattainable. Those who maintain that their feelings concerning things somehow reveal reality will interact toward the events of life unrealistically as if they were in a dream. Many aspects of the New Age Movement epitomize this approach.

The intellectual position is similarly distanced from the event but it is a qualitatively different stance than feeling-sentience that relies heavily upon systematic rationale. But a cerebral faculty is not an entity but a reasoning agency. It does not possess singular identity any more than the heart or the lung and, consequently, without a self, it cannot engage phenomena and circumstances experientially.

Immediate cognition requires the direct engagement of the human quiddity, otherwise heightened cognition through the human, feeling condition or the intellect is not a real advance in terms of definitive knowledge. It is the incorporeal identity that alone is able to experience the authentic state of existence of things because the human quiddity resides in an original, elemental condition.

The distinction between the conventional practices

of cognition and immediate engagement rests upon the perspective from which phenomena are encountered. The manner whereby the conclusive condition of identity of something is discovered requires that the authentic identity of the human being be established as the sovereign singularity and view-point from which all things are directly engaged.

If someone is convinced that the body or more specifically, the brain, is the extent of their identity, they will remain unpersuaded of a need to experientially investigate and discover their own authentic existence. They will not suspect that the elemental condition in which the human quiddity exists offers a perspective towards phenomena whereby definitive knowledge is readily apprehensible.

Similarly, if it is imagined that how we feel is what we are, then we remain limited to the stifling perspective of feeling-sentience which is a condition only a little remote from that of the animal.

The impetus and incentive towards the empirical exploration of the authentic identity of the human being must be the attainment of definite knowledge concerning the actual condition of things. An honest examination of our conventional cognitive approaches would most certainly reveal a significant lack of conclusive knowledge. In many cases it is blatantly evident that we neither know what we are doing and certainly not who we are. Everywhere we cast a glance, we recognize the consequences of existential ignorance and there is no respite except in the experiential discovery of our authentic identities and the establishment of a perspective from our sovereign autonomy towards all other circumstances. Through this means alone we attain both definitive knowledge and self-determination.

17. CONCLUSIVE KNOWLEDGE

Knowledge concerning the authentic condition of existence is achieved through original engagement by the quiddity of our own existence. If a representation purports to portray something that otherwise only exists intangibly, it will be recognizable to the degree that it is explicitly depicted and will be further dependent upon our own capacity to interpret the particular medium of expression.

In terms of an artistic representation, therefore, the content of the work is of supreme importance just as the significance of a Natural phenomenon lies within a similarly intangible merit. We cannot discover the essential content of an artwork, that of a plant or creature or even another human being, unless approach it directly without imagining that we already know what it is.

The term, direct engagement immediately poses the necessity to establish a distinction between our corporeally established condition and our essential identity. If we encounter something immediately through our understanding and feelings concerning it, we achieve nothing unusual. While, customarily, we identify with the human body, unaware that it is merely the superficial representation of an intangible significance of existence, experientially, we are able to discover the authentic condition through the restraint of our corporeal faculties and feeling nature. When these faculties are contained, that which remains is readily recognized as our authentic existence.

The significance of direct cognition rests upon the establishment of the human, singularity of existence as the sovereign perspective of perception. The manner whereby the human quiddity engages the elemental condition of phenomena is immediate and experiential.

Through the incorporeal distinction of the human quiddity, every phenomenal experience may be identified for its intrinsic significance because the essential existence of the human being is not embroiled in the physical state. In this sense, the human quiddity is able to remain entirely objective and discern the actual, existential condition of things. It experiences phenomena at their most elemental because it exists in the same essential and profound condition. The state in which the human quiddity and the essential of all other phenomena exists is not a mysterious or outlandish circumstance but it is the opposite situation to the superficial.

In the light of direct cognition, the merely physical representation is recognized as cursory. This can be readily illustrated in terms of interpersonal interactions. If another human being is merely considered a physical object then a meaningful exchange is impossible. Additionally, if one individual is convinced that the extent of their own existence is merely corporeal, they will only engage with the physically blatant condition of another person. It is when the essential person is recognized and respected that effective and meaningful communication is possible.

To extend the example further, if an individual is subjectively encountered, merely in terms of our particular preferences and predilections, once more we fail to see the actual individual and merely encounter a reflection of our own idiosyncrasies and biases. Thus, through the distortion of our own character we obscure the reality of the other person.

If we immediately engage another human being through the aegis of our own singular distinction of existence, we discover their essential condition in much the same way as we determine the elemental condition of existence of any phenomenon. When we encounter something directly through the quiddity of our existence we find the substantial and meaningful that epitomizes it. We engage the quintessential significance that signifies its actuality. We discover the essential condition of its existence.

In terms of meeting another human being we may interact superficially or recognize the elemental condition of the human entity through our own similarly essential distinction. When a phenomenon is engaged in this manner, its substantial condition becomes evident and we are aware that we are engaging something on completely different terms than usual. We recognize, that formerly we only addressed the unidimensional aspects of the appearance while now we engage the full amplitude of its existence and we discover the intrinsic condition that exemplifies its identity.

When we engage another human directly in this manner we discern something more. We find that their essential existence is beyond reproach. We recognize that it is the presuppositional limitations that we impose that hinder a legitimate view of another human being and, recognizing their essential condition, we experience a consequent deference that is an event of inviolable love.

This event reveals the inherent nature of essential existence It is certainly not subjectively experienced because it does not involve sentiment. It is something that is discovered only when the human quiddity immediately encounters the essential condition of another person. We recognize that this event of knowledge is not founded upon our feeling-sentient nature and that it is not intellectually approached. It is evident to us that this is something that we could never discover through conventional cognition.

Through the confusion between sentiment and comity we entirely underestimate the significance of mutual deference as the essential condition of existence. We discover its authenticity only through the perspective of our own singular distinction. It remains illusive to us through our conventional cognitive practices. We certainly do not experience deference when we engage other human beings and phenomena superficially.

Through our corporeally established faculties and

feeling-sentient nature, we are unable to recognize the essential condition of things. We perceive phenomena in part without their qualitative value and intrinsic significance. Only the human quiddity is able to determine the incorporeal substance of phenomena and the deferential nature whereby existence is essentially composed. When the quiddity is recognized through immediate engagement and established as the sovereign perspective of the human being, it is found that it inhabits a state of authenticity. The qualitative nature of existential reality is discovered to exist in a manner that is both good and beautiful. We further recognized that it is the encumbrance of an essentially superficial perspective towards existence that prevents us from immediate experiencing the full extent of Aristotelean entelechy.

Immediate cognition requires a non-cerebral, unemotional dexterity whereby the direct engagement of a circumstance is attentively encountered by the human, singular distinction. The essential condition of a phenomenon is engaged directly and experientially, uninfluenced by evaluational prejudice. Similarly, the qualitative value of a thing is discovered without recourse to pre-established assessment. This important prerequisite allows the human quiddity to experience something originally and discover through acute attention the intrinsic significance and condition of existence of the phenomenon.

The manner whereby the essential distinction that

identifies a phenomenon is discovered resembles the approach of the artist who experientially engages an intangible condition and endeavors to articulate it through an appropriate artistic medium. The artist struggles to represent something that remains otherwise unapparent. The elusive element is grasped through direct experience and the intrinsic significance of something is thereby discovered. An extant, yet intangible value is represented through metaphoric and figurative means in order that it may be successfully perceived by the spectator.

This is a vastly different approach to the artisan-craftsman. The craftsman fabricates an item beautifully but not in an attempt to articulate an intangible content. Something is made that is functional, utilitarian or decorative and appealingly fashioned.

Nowadays, the distinction between art and craft has become muddled. Thus, we have competent artisans who contend that their work is art with an ensuing upswing of the dilettante commodity, masquerading as if it were revealing something of intangible significance. While such work elicits the marginal interest of the curious, serious damage follows when museum and gallery director remain ignorant of the misconception, because it diminishes the value and significance of authentic, artistic revelation.

Similarly, philosophical authority that is founded merely upon the material appearances and the physical properties of phenomena, reduces the essential significance of existence to a superficial and meaningless representation. In order to productively advance beyond the shallow and vacuous restrains of an exclusively materialistic philosophy, it is necessary to explore a superior cognitive approach. This is achievable through the establishment of an antithetic perspective towards existence through the experiential recognition of the human quiddity.

Other Books by the Same Author

TOWARDS A MEANINGFUL FUTURE
The Continuum of the Qualitative Expansion of the Soul

THE IMMANENT PRINCIPLE OF INTEGRITY AND GOODWILL
The Integration of the Principle of Virtue within the Human heart

THE EVOLUTIONARY IMPERATIVE OF OUR TIME
The Crucial Establishment of an Inspired Ethos with the Individual, Human Heart, appropriate to a Meaningful Future

RECONCILIATION WITH HUMAN DESTINY
The Surrender of the Heart-of-the-Soul as the Expedient Approach Towards Direct Engagement with the Immanent Exemplar of a Future, Human Disposition

THE QUALITATIVE EVOLUTION OF THE SOUL
The Evolutionary Transformation of the Human Soul Through Openhearted Sincerity Towards Immanent Caritas

THE SUPERNAL ETHOS
Unanimity with the Divine Nature

THE BEGINNING OF WISDOM
Knowledge through Immediate Engagement

UNDER THE AEGIS OF IMMANENT CARITAS
The Reorientation of the Human, Disparate Self-circumscribed Mentality

THE DECEPTION OF MATERIALISTIC WESTERN PHILOSOPHY
An Exploration of the Physically Elusive Volume of Existence

THE MEANINGFUL VOLUME OF EXISTENCE
An Exploration of the Overlooked Intangible Significance of Phenomena

THE OBSOLETE SELF
Individual Uniqueness and Significance beyond Egocentrism

HUMAN SOVEREIGN AUTONOMY
The Discovery of the Human Ipseity and its Establishment as the Essential Authority of the Human Constitution

THE TRANSFORMATION OF THE SOUL
From Self-Centeredness to Sovereign Autonomy

THE IMPLICATION OF HUMAN, INCORPOREAL EXISTENCE
The Overlooked Significance of the Intangible and Qualitative Dimension of Existence

IMMEDIATE EXPERIENTIAL COGNITION
The Inherent Human Capacity of Immediate Engagement

THE HUMAN ESSENTIAL IDENTITY
Direct Experience of Intangible Significance

KNOWLEDGE THROUGH DIRECT COGNITION
The Human Conscious Individuality and Immediately Experienced Reality

www.ingramcontent.com/pod-product-compliance
Lightning Source LLC
Chambersburg PA
CBHW070809100426
42742CB00012B/2308